YOU'RE HIRED! INTERVIEW

TIPS & TECHNIQUES FOR A BRILLIANT INTERVIEW

JUDI JAMES

You're Hired! Interview: tips & techniques for a brilliant interview

This first edition published in 2009 by Trotman Publishing, a division of Crimson Publishing Ltd., Westminster House, Kew Road, Richmond, Surrey TW9 2ND

Author Judi James

British Library Cataloguing in Publication Data
A catalogue record for this book is available from the British Library

ISBN 978 1 84455 178 1

Designed by Nicki Averill
Typeset by RefineCatch Ltd, Bungay, Suffolk
Printed and bound in Great Britain by TJ International Ltd, Padstow, Comwall

CONTENTS

ABOUT THE AUTHOR

A leading author with 20 published book titles, including *BodyTalk at Work*, plus regular advice/analysis columns in magazines like *Zest*, *More*, *You* and *Heat*, Judi is also a TV expert in the field of body language and behaviour, having had her own series *Naked Celebrity*, plus her own nightly slot on Ch5 News during the general election, as well as appearing regularly on *Big Brother on the Couch*.

Judi is also a high-profile name in the corporate field with 15 years' experience running training courses across the UK and speaking at keynote conferences. She has spent several years talking to school leavers about job interview techniques and she has also fronted a government-sponsored adult learning campaign, talking about the psychology of learning and emotional issues involved.

INTRODUCTION

Are you a masochist, an egomaniac or an attention-seeking show-off?

If you answered 'no' to all the above, the chances are you don't enjoy job interviews.

For most people hunting for work, the interview is about as much fun as chewing off your own elbow. For the compulsive show-off with narcissistic tendencies it might be viewed as an opportunity to excel, but for the rest of us the thought of packaging up our flimsy self-esteem and presenting it to a stranger to trample into the shag-pile at will can be perfectly horrible.

The good news is that you *can* learn to love interviews. Even if this book doesn't make interviews one of the greatest pleasures of your life, right up there along with the likes of buying your first Porsche or eating chocolate – it *will* help to make the process easier and more enjoyable, as well as ensuring your interview outcomes are far more successful.

This book is a practical, informative and fun guide for anyone facing recruitment or promotional interviews, whether you're a first or second-jobber, career-changer or even someone who is returning to work after a break.

An interview is a both a ritual *and* a performance. We'll be looking at the simple steps of getting the rituals right – learning how to meet, greet, dress and impress – and then the inspirational and truly liberating techniques of overcoming nerves, shyness and lack of confidence to ensure you allow yourself to shine. There will be practical tips on CVs and preparation, plus advice on handling questions, from the simplest to the trickiest. There will even be a chapter on après-interview follow-ups.

We'll approach all these skills with energy, commitment and humour. Why humour? Because it's the one thing that keeps you going when the energy and commitment are in danger of running out of juice. Laughter is your all-important self-defence system. We use it to diminish our fears and our enemies, and when you start to take yourself too seriously during your interview experience you put out the 'Welcome' mat to anxiety, debilitating nervousness, low self-esteem and even paranoia. Professionalism doesn't have to be too po-faced and some of my funniest stories come under the heading of: 'Dreadful interviews I have been on in my life'.

'You grow up the day you have the first real laugh at yourself'
Ethel Barrymore

Learning to love interviews: rule 1

Don't let them scare you!

An interview should be challenging, stimulating and only *mildly* daunting. It *ought* to bring out the best in you, not the worst. It's an opportunity, not a battle. The interviewer wants you to be just as brilliant as you do. He or she is there hoping to spot talent and potential, not to scythe an applicant's legs from under them. Don't scupper your own opportunities by negative thinking. Like sporting success or stage performance, your mental attitude will be just as crucial to your success as your abilities and experience.

This book aims to keep you fired up and buoyant throughout every stage of your interview process. At times it will feel like an encouraging pat on the back and at others more like a firm kick up the bum! You'll be learning DIY motivational skills to keep you focused and upbeat, even in the face of possible disappointment and turn-downs. It will ensure your determination to succeed is far greater than your determination to fail. All you need to keep in mind right now is the following inspirational message to yourself:

Learning to love interviews: rule 2

Allow yourself to shine!

You are unique. You have talents, skills and quality of character. Your potential is limitless. Not every company you apply to will be looking for your type of uniqueness, which is why you'll need to expand your skill and experience base to improve your chances. And not every organisation will get the real 'you', which is why it's vital to present yourself in a way that works in a relatively short space of time.

Learning to love interviews: rule 3

Never take advice from someone in difficulties!

Advice is cheap and – when you're preparing for your interview – it can be pelted and lobbed at you from all sides like rotten fruit, but remember not all of it should be heeded, let alone acted upon. Much of it will come from people to whom success is such a complete and utter stranger they wouldn't recognise it if it came at them wearing a bowler hat and sporting a large pink carnation in its lapel. In fact, many of the most well worn words of interview 'wisdom' are so completely inadequate that if I were a lawyer I'd be suing them for criminal negligence.

Want to know three of the dumbest pieces of advice you'll ever hear when you go to a job interview?

- Just be yourself.
- You can only do your best.
- If it's meant to be it's meant to be.

Sound familiar?

The problem with advice like this is that it all points to one main hypothesis: 'Why bother?' All three statements are designed to seduce you into inertia or idleness by implying the interview outcome is reassuringly out of your hands. This lack of perceivable control means it's not your fault if you fail, which is the brain's damage-limitation exercise aimed at protecting your self-esteem. Put any proper effort in and you start to accept liability for any failure. Better to sit back and *hope* the interview panel will like you than to take any steps to acquire the kind of skills that might ensure they approve.

Learning to love interviews: rule 4

You're only as strong as your weakest *think*

Imagine applying these previous mantras to another core skill you've learned in your life, like driving a car. You get in for your first lesson and your instructor tells you that 'If it's meant to be it's meant to be'. If you're lucky enough to get the motor running in the first place the 'just be yourself' tip will probably have you losing control and skidding straight into the nearest lamp-post. So here's some quick advice about those three key messages.

- **Just be yourself.** This is impossible and impractical. An interview is a formal process, during which you will be asked to sell yourself and your abilities to one or a group of strangers. Is this behaviour part of your normal daily life? Do you have a 'self' for this situation? The answer is probably 'No'.
- **You can only do your best.** How do you know? You have no idea what your best is. We are all capable of wonderful and extraordinary things, well beyond our own bounds of comprehension. There should be no false lid on your achievements.
- **If it's meant to be it's meant to be.** Since when did you turn into a hippie, allowing cosmic fate to rule your life? Take control, pronto. It's up to you to decide how well you're going to do, not karma. Or as someone once said: 'The harder I work, the luckier I seem to get.'

Suck it and see?

Many of the key events in your life that prompted massive change – like falling in love, getting pregnant (or getting *someone* pregnant) or buying a house or flat – probably happened quite quickly, and the performance known as going on an interview can be the same. For a few minutes' exchange of information you could end up with a career or job that will change the course of your entire life. Yet many applicants are happy to pitch up without preparation, planning or even clear targets or objectives. They work on a process of 'suck it and see', i.e. they turn up and play it by ear.

Do you believe you have no control over your own destiny? Do you *really* think that the best advice before attending an interview is 'just be yourself'? Or do you think that success is something that anyone can achieve thanks to effort, focus and the odd pinch of good luck?

This book is all about those last three qualities, but primarily the first two. It's for people who believe that: 'The harder I work the luckier I seem to get.' Or, as Ralph Waldo Emerson said: 'Shallow men believe in luck, strong men believe in cause and effect.' It's about optimism and change rather than sitting back and moaning about how life never deals you a winning hand. Remember, any idiot can moan and whinge – and most idiots do!

How to use this book

Your skills at interview level will consist of five key 'layers', which you can visualise as the layers of an large onion that has been cut in half (but without the tears!).

Layer 1: qualified skills

This layer consists of your certified and measured skills, i.e. your qualifications. You will have presented these in your CV before you attend an interview. If you're applying for promotion, you might need to add any qualifications gained during your present employment with the company.

Layer 2: job experience

This layer consists of your work or work-related experience. These details should also have been logged on your CV and will probably be discussed during the interview. They can include unpaid voluntary work or temporary employment as well as regular employment. If you're returning to work after an absence, you should consider logging work-experience like bringing up a family or running a home.

Layer 3: personal talent

This is formed by your personality and behaviour skills. Are you loyal, punctual, diligent or caring? Do you have teambuilding or management abilities? Can you motivate or entertain? How confident are you? What is your self-esteem like?

Layer 4: psychometric tests

These would be any skills that are tested during the interview process with things like maths or written tests.

Layer 5: soft skills

These are the communication or performance skills that you will display during your interview process. They include visual, verbal and vocal communications and your ability to navigate through meeting and greeting, listening and informing. It will include your ability to chat and do small talk, answer questions about yourself and your experience, values and overall employment skills.

Interpersonal skills are vital in modern business, and what are known as **soft skills** are highly in demand. The ability to relate well to other people is so important that, when Microsoft asked UK business leaders what the most sought-after skills were, teamworking and interpersonal skills topped the list. Your interpersonal skills will be assessed to judge whether you have the ability to communicate with other employees, persuade and influence clients, and manage or lead teams.

Layers 1–3 will be part of your career pre-planning and primarily dealt with way before interview stage, although there will be advice throughout this book in shoring up possible gaps for future interviews. Layers 4 and 5 will form the heart of this book, with a large wad of advice added to help you deal with any nerves or lack of confidence both before and during your performance stages.

There will be pre-work that you can use for preparation but there will also be quick-fix tips on each stage of your interviews plus a 'Troubleshooting' section with emergency advice, should you need it.

So here's the core mantra of this book repeated again:

Allow yourself to shine!

It's the one key discipline you're going to need. Because with the help of this book, it's not just your shoes you're going to be polishing before your next interview, it's your presentation, your personality and your performance. We're going to work on the basis that to fail to prepare is to prepare to fail, meaning any effort and strategy planning work you put in before your interview can only be a good thing. We'll also be looking at the fact that charm and natural charisma might take you a long way in life, but only if you know how to exude them!

1 WHY INTERVIEWS?

This chapter will help you understand the aims and purpose of your interviews by:

- explaining why your face-to-face skills are so vital for your career success
- showing the role of the interviewer and the four key aims he or she will have during your interview
- explaining the difference between a good interview and a bad one
- widening the scope of the interview process by warning when it actually *does* start as well as finish!
- looking at the structure of an interview
- outlining all the different types of interview that you might encounter.

Why interviews? Sounds obvious, doesn't it? But it could be argued that an interview is a subjective way of making what should be an objective decision. After all, if you have someone's details and qualifications and they've all been checked out thoroughly, why would you need to see the candidate as well? Particularly as visual impressions are famously unreliable!

With the current passion for impersonal communication it's possible for companies to tiptoe a long way up the recruitment path without having to use the evidence of their eyes. Most interviews have a telephone stage and many will also involve email. A lot will also employ psychometric testing (sets of written or online questions to judge your personality and behaviour traits) to come up with what should be an unbiased evaluation. Did you know some companies have even dabbled with internet recruitment, using sites like Second Life to set up virtual recruitment fairs that end in a real-life job? Or that companies will often Google applicants or look them up on social sites like Facebook to see if they're quite as personable and charming as they sound on their CV?

The heavy costs involved in both time and money spent during the selection process mean that pressure on interviewers to hire the right candidate is intense, leading to stress on both sides. Employers are always looking for ways to recruit star employees using the quickest, easiest and most cost-effective but foolproof methods possible. Every time they recruit a 'wrong 'un' they know their own reputation or even career is at risk. But all this impersonal and highly factual ducking and diving will only delay the inevitable. At some stage in the recruitment process the dog is going to have to see the rabbit, meaning you will find yourself sitting in front of a desk or around a table, face-to-face with your interviewer or interview panel.

The problem for interviewers is that it would be extremely difficult to employ someone without having met them first.

I asked several professional recruitment interviewers why they liked to see an applicant before making a job offer. Here's a selection of their replies.

- 'If the job is customer-facing I need to see how they present in person. Are they personable and well-groomed? It's only really when we see them in the flesh that we can judge them in the same way as our customers.'

- 'I always read through the CV before an interview but I believe you can tell more about someone's personality by looking at them.'
- 'Sometimes candidates lie or exaggerate on their CV. If I question them face-to-face I can get to the truth.'
- 'I need to see if they'll fit into the company culture.'
- 'I always think the body language is very telling.'
- 'Image is important for our company. We wouldn't want to hire someone who dressed inappropriately.'
- 'We count interpersonal techniques as one of the core skills for any job in this company. It's not enough that they can speak well over the phone or submit a good written CV, we also need to see that they can interact in a face-to-face scenario.'
- 'People bluff their way into jobs. A good interviewer will get to the truth though.'
- 'You look for moments of hesitation or uncertainty that let you know you need to probe more.'

When does an interview start?

It's easy to assume that an interview starts the moment you walk into the interviewer's office and he or she begins to ask you questions. But in many ways this isn't a stage production. Things don't only kick off when the house lights go down and the curtains go up. Your interview will have started the moment you first contacted the company or agency. Every communication can be seen as part of the evaluation process. There are at least 11 basic stages that you should consider to be part of the process that is called **The Interview**:

1. telephone or email contact to apply or get details
2. company recruitment events
3. your CV
4. arrival and wait in reception
5. pick up and small talk
6. being questioned by the interviewer
7. a 'walk the job' (being shown around the company to visit sites and employees)
8. lunch or other meal taken on the premises
9. tests and tasks
10. your thank-you note or follow-up contact
11. any re-call interviews.

Oh, and if you're attending an internal promotion interview you will be aware that your interview process began the moment you started work in your company, won't you? No matter how many years ago that was. (No pressure!)

What makes a bad interview?

Bad interviews aren't just the ones that don't end with a job offer. In fact it's entirely feasible (and common) to find you've been offered a job that you're tempted to turn down purely because the interview was so dire. In fact, a survey of more than 2,000 people on behalf of T-Mobile found that a third of job applicants come away from an interview with a bad impression of the business. Consulting firm Development Dimensions report that a bad interview experience would influence the decision of two-thirds of jobseekers whether to accept an offer or not.

Bad interviews range from the mildly off-putting:

- 'They made me wait over half an hour in a packed reception and the interviewer didn't even apologise for the delay.'
- 'The interviewer was off sick and I think they'd roped her assistant in at the last minute.'

To the downright disgusting:

- 'I had to meet the HR woman in a City bar. She acted as though she'd been drinking already.'
- 'They got my name wrong and kept referring to the wrong CV.'
- 'He sat on the floor behind his desk and asked me to get his interest.'
- 'The boss kept asking me how I'd cope if I had children.'

What makes a good interview?

Good interviews, like bad ones, can come in all shapes and sizes but you'll usually be left feeling satisfied if:

- you're given sufficient time to talk and not felt rushed
- you're asked challenging but appropriate questions

SHAME ON THEM!

A survey by Reed Business Information discovered 1 in 10 HR professionals admitted they had lied while applying for a job!

- you're listened to
- your interviewer knows your name and has read your CV thoroughly
- there is more than one person interviewing – to make the selection process less subjective
- you're treated politely and punctually
- you're made to feel at ease
- you're given information about the company and about the job you're applying for
- you're treated with fairness
- you're informed when to expect a decision.

THINGS TO ENJOY IN YOUR INTERVIEW

- Knowing the interviewer is likely to be just as nervous as you are, if not more nervous – after all his or her reputation/job might be at stake if they fail to come up with the goods.
- Getting dressed up. It's good to see yourself in a smart suit now and again.
- Imagining the interviewer in the nude/on the toilet. It's one of the oldest tricks in the book when it comes to making yourself feel more at ease. I'm not sure it really works but it should bring a smile to your face!
- Telling complete strangers about all your achievements without being accused of boasting.
- Playing 'interview catchphrase bingo'. How long before they say 'We have other candidates to see'; 'Here's a potted history of the company'; 'Did you have any trouble finding us?'; or 'I've read through your CV of course but I'd like you to tell me about yourself'.
- Saying 'I'll get my coat' when the interviewer asks why your Facebook name is 'Skankyhotchick.com'.

How the purpose of an interview is structured

Let's start by making things simple. There are four key aims of any good recruitment or promotion interview.

1. **Prediction:** to select the right person for the job or promotion.
2. **Education:** to give out information about the job.
3. **Influencing and persuading:** to get the right candidate to accept the job.
4. **Image and public relations (PR):** to create a good image of the company whether you intend to recruit the candidate or not.

WHAT DO MOST WORKERS WANT FROM A JOB?

A Towers Perrin 2007–2008 Global Workforce Study suggests the following:

- competitive base pay
- career advancement opportunities
- convenient work location
- flexible schedule
- learning and development opportunities
- generous holiday allowance
- organisation's reputation as a good employer
- reasonable workload
- organisation's financial health.

How your role relates to this structure

Your own prime objective will be to get that job or promotion. However, your role in each of the four key aims listed above does need to be active rather than passive, which means you'll be trying to show the following.

- **Qualifications and experience:** to present yourself as the best person for the job.
- **Listening and questioning skills:** to get more information about the job.
- **Personality, behaviour, communication skills and emotional intelligence:** to persuade and influence them to make an offer.
- **Personal PR and marketing:** to create a positive impression for the future, even if you don't get an offer this time.

HOW EASY IS IT TO FIND THE RIGHT RECRUITS?

The Chartered Institute of Personnel Development (CIPD) 2007 survey on recruitment, retention and turnover found that 45% of organisations found managerial and professional roles difficult to fill and 25% struggle to fill senior management posts.

84% of organisations struggle to recruit new people and the most frequent method of addressing this issue is to appoint people who don't match the job criteria but who show potential to grow into the role.

Ready? Willing? Able?

To make things even simpler, keep in mind that most interviewers will be checking you out for three key things at interview stage.

1. **Ready?** Do you have enough experience for the job? Can you fit in with the rest of the team or department?
2. **Willing?** Will you bring enthusiasm, energy, commitment and hard work to the role?
3. **Able**? Do you have the skills and qualifications for the job?

Perhaps everyone who is successful enough to reach interview level is rich in all three qualities. In this case, the interviewer's job will be to discover who is richest.

Or it could be that nobody fits the bill perfectly. Then – instead of allowing the best to go through – the interviewer might be looking to weigh competencies up against each other. In this case, any lack of previous experience might be weighed against keenness and enthusiasm to learn. So a weakness in one category might not be fatal if you're stronger in another.

Microsoft asked 500 UK business leaders what the most sought-after skills were. Team working and interpersonal skills topped the list.

Or it *might* be that they're struggling to get anyone to apply and will just pick the first person who walks through the door (this might sound funny but I've spoken to companies with this dilemma).

Or ... it could be something in between any of the above.

Types of interview

One-to-one recruitment interview

A bog-standard recruitment interview might take up to an hour, during which you'll be asked questions from either a company owner (in the case of a smaller firm), department manager or human resources manager. Many of the questions will relate to your CV, which you will have sent to them beforehand as part of the pre-interview selection stage.

Interviewers vary in the way they conduct an interview. Some will stick to a formal style, with set questions that they will ask everyone. Others prefer a casual style that is more conversational. Expect to be shown into an office, introduced to the interviewer and offered tea or coffee. There should be some small talk and then he or she will ask you some job-related questions. At the end of the interview you shouldn't expect to hear whether you've got the job or not but you should expect to be informed when and how you will be notified.

Panel interview

This can be very similar to the interview above in format, except you'll be greeted and questioned by more than one person. There could be as many as six people on the panel and they might not all participate in the question and answer session. The idea of being interviewed by a panel might sound more intimidating but it's done largely for your benefit – to guarantee a fair and objective selection process.

Hi-tech interview

This is an interview that is conducted long-distance, either over the telephone or via video-conferencing. A webcam might be used to interview over the Internet or you could be called into a local branch of the firm to use their telephone or video-conferencing facilities. This type of interviewing is becoming more common but rarely as a standalone. It's more likely done as part of the pre-selection process and will usually lead up to a face-to-face interview.

Psychometric testing

Psychometric tests are more likely to be part of the overall interview process and as such tend to fall into two different categories.

1. **Aptitude tests:** designed to test your skills for the job, such as numeracy or logic skills.
2. **Personality tests:** ask about your behaviours and thoughts in specific situations.

Both can be written tests or completed online.

Presentation

There's a possibility you could be asked to present, which means you will put together a more formal talk to the panel which will be uninterrupted, with the question session at the end. This might sound daunting but there is advice in later chapters to make this easy for you. In many ways, it's like giving you a clear run at pitching for the job, allowing you time to put forward all your appropriate qualifications and skills. Presentations are rarely – if ever – requested off the cuff and you will be aware that it's expected of you before you turn up. If you're attending a first job interview and have no university or career experience, it's very unlikely you'll be asked to give a presentation.

Assessment centres

You may be interviewed at an assessment centre, usually run by an external company, which has been hired by the company that is recruiting. This might be held at an actual centre, in a hotel or even at the company's own premises. If they're external, these centres specialise in recruitment interviewing on behalf of other companies. They will conduct your interview, then feed their findings back to the company itself. The main objective of an assessment centre is to evaluate your skills and aptitude for a job by testing them out, rather than going on written or verbal proof. Expect role-plays, teambuilding and/or leadership tasks.

Recruitment agencies

If you apply for work through a recruitment agency, you will have your first interview with the agency, who will act as a selection filter before sending you to any firm recruiting in your field of work. These agencies get many applicants and there is advice later in the book about getting your face known to them to ensure you get the pick of the best jobs.

Second interview

If your first interview is successful, you should be informed via post or email. Then you will either be made a formal offer or you'll be asked back for another interview. If you're asked back, it is either part of the normal process or because there are more than one of the first-batch applicants who are suitable for the post and they're whittling the final few candidates down. It's likely a lot of their questions during any second interview will be clarifying information you gave during the first interview.

This chapter acts as a preview, giving you an overall look at things you can generally expect at an interview. As Corporal Jones always says in *Dad's Army*:

Don't panic!

There is advice in this book to get your through all or any of these interview stages. None of them is hard, although each will come with its own degree of difficulty. Difficulty is good for you! If you never take on anything that's difficult you'll never allow yourself to stretch and grow.

The only thing worse than a difficult interview is an easy one. Getting a good job should create feelings of achievement. An interview that's like a walk in the park should send out warning signals. Any interviewer who doesn't ask challenging questions is either disinterested, unprofessional or desperate!

IN A NUTSHELL

- Remember your key roles: presentation, information (giving and gathering), persuasion (getting them to want to employ you) and making a positive impression for future consideration.
- Prepare your pitch, keeping in mind the interviewer's three prime areas of interest. Are you: **Ready? Willing?** and **Able** to do the job?
- There are several different types of interview. Which is yours? Planning and preparation is all about honing the right techniques for the right type of meeting.

2 ASSESSING THE PRODUCT

What is it I have to sell?

All recruitment or internal promotion interviews are about selling and yet many applicants arrive unprepared for any form of self-marketing and self-presentation. In a job interview *you* are the product under discussion, and this chapter will help you to market yourself in the most positive and successful way by:

- recognising and prioritising your strengths
- taking an objective view of your skills and talents
- seeing what will sell and what won't
- building up your 'Shield' to create competence and confidence
- being aware of the scope of your competencies by studying the 'Eight Intelligences'.

You and your self

All communication begins with the **self**, which means your self-image and self-belief about who you are and what your standing is in the world at large. In your interview communications there are four 'selves' in play:

1. your self-belief and self-image
2. your impression and thoughts of your interviewer
3. their status and self-image
4. their impression of you.

This is where image management comes in. During your interview, you'll need to sell yourself, using a firm amount of self-belief and a positive expectation of your interviewer's impression of you to create a 'sale'. The first stage of that sale is to learn how to evaluate and then market the product, which is you.

OK, so the idea of selling yourself might sound a bit drastic, after all, as Patrick McGoohan famously said in his cult TV series *The Prisoner*: 'I am not a number, I'm a free man!' But although a career might not mean selling your soul or even your body, it certainly means selling your talents, skills, time, energy and commitment.

Your first step before even applying for an interview, then, is to take a good, hard look at all of this vast pool of talent and ability. After all, it's what you'll be hawking and – like any good salesman – you should have plenty of product knowledge.

Chocolate delight

Do you know much about marketing techniques? For the sake of this exercise, I'd like you to think of yourself as a chocolate bar that is being newly launched on the market (or re-launched if you're a returner to work). Selling that chocolate will be all about five key things.

1. **Product information:** how does it look and taste?
2. **Product packaging:** what kind of wrapper will it have?
3. **Market platform:** to whom might this chocolate appeal most?

4. **Price:** is it value for money?
5. **Advertising**: how can it be presented in a way that sells?

All of these will apply to your own marketing skills.

- **Product information:** What are my skills and talents?
- **Packaging:** What should I wear to the interview? How should I look and sound?
- **Market platform:** What type of company or job will create the best career 'fit'?
- **Price:** What do I expect to be paid?
- **Advertising:** How do I let them know I'm here?

Simple, basic good sense really, isn't it?

Creating your Shield

To help firm up this product knowledge you're going to create your Shield. This Shield will be your armour, force field and even defence and protection as you work your way through the job market. It will also help you apply for the right type of jobs, rather than just scattering your talents to the winds and hoping something takes seed. Your interview might be all-important to you right now, but it's only the first stage in what could be a very long career trail, so some focused and directional thinking is vital.

The Shield is an amazingly effective feelgood exercise, because it is a very simple and even enjoyable way to do all of the following as you prepare for your interviews. The Shield will:

- boost your confidence
- help you to compile your CV
- help you construct your jobseeking strategies
- ensure you sell yourself to the maximum during interviews
- highlight any areas of weakness that could be worked on prior to the interview
- help you see that you are an all-round wonderful person
- make you feel more like a warrior than a wimp as you approach the job market!

ACTIVITY 1

BUILD YOUR SHIELD

Take a large piece of paper, preferably A4 or bigger.

Using up most of the page, draw the shape of a shield or – if your artistic talents aren't really keeping Lucien Freud awake at night – just divide the paper into four squares.

The quadrants of your Shield

Hard skills	Soft skills
Achievements	Personality

Write a heading at the top of each quadrant:

hard skills
soft skills
achievements
personality

Fill in each quadrant, making as long a list as possible.

Hard skills

These are any qualifications you have or other practical abilities such as driving, using a computer or speaking other languages. Most of these will be measurable, but not necessarily. If you can do it, write it down and don't self-censor. You're not making comparisons, you're compiling a profile of yourself. This is the place to be objective, not modest or humble. Go back to those marketing guys sitting around their board table discussing ways of selling that chocolate bar. Do you think the conversation goes like this?

> 'It tastes great, I suppose.'
> 'Yeah, lots of cocoa solids. Consumers like that.'
> 'But not as many as those rival brands so maybe we shouldn't mention them at all.'
> 'It's not quite as big as the rival bar, either. And it's not really as creamy. Let's not say anything at all about taste, size or cocoa solids then, just in case.'
> 'No, when you're marketing every plus point is a plus point and any minus points can be plus points, too! Take this dialogue for example.'
> 'It's more expensive than all the other brands by a mile.'
> 'Hey, that's great! We've got a luxury chocolate bar for genuine indulgence. Buy it because you're worth it, or buy it to show your girlfriend you really care.'

So if you can swim, write it down. Don't leave this skill off the list just because everyone else you know can swim better than you do.

Soft skills

These are the behaviour and interpersonal skills you have, and which many recruiters value higher than the hard skills. To help you with your list, I've created a word-buffet to whet your appetite and start your selection. Are you good at any of the following?

listening
communicating
using the telephone
handling customers
giving advice or help
coaching
mentoring
managing
leadership
time management
being assertive
motivating
selling
teambuilding
persuading and influencing
negotiating
delegating
presenting to groups
training
handling difficult people

If you're returning to work, or a late starter because you've been bringing up a family, you can happily apply these skills to your home and social life. Being a parent requires competency in many of these basic soft skills and it will help if you can use **transcribed thinking**: looking at skills you use in one place and seeing how they would apply in another.

One of the toughest types to negotiate with is a small child. Children make the toughest, best negotiators. Why? Because they're as focused as an Exocet missile when it comes to getting what they want. They have no shame about techniques for getting it, and they won't give up until they're successful. If you've had any success at all in your negotiations with your 3-year-old, you'll find handling that chief exec in the boardroom a doddle!

How crafty are you at getting your own way at home? And how time-managed do you have to be? Do you find yourself being assertive rather than shouting the odds when things go wrong? And do you have a daily task of delegation?

If you struggle seeing these daily skills in context, do invest in a couple of business books that aim at teaching you all these soft skills. Once you start to evaluate them in this way, I promise your next thought will be: 'but that's just basic common sense!' Of course it is, but never underestimate good old common sense. It's as rare as hens' teeth in the business world. I know because I've been selling nothing but for years!

Achievements

Any achievement is only as great as the effort and resolve taken to do it. I'm telling you this because this section of the Shield needs to be very personal. What have you done in your life that took effort? What personal challenge have you overcome? A true achievement is something that you will have felt like patting your own back for, even if there wasn't a brass band waiting once you'd done it.

I've achieved many things in my life, from getting books published to having my own TV series, but my *greatest* achievement was getting into a lift at Canary Wharf and taking it to the top floor. Why? Because I suffer from claustrophobia and had not been in a lift for 15 years. It took more courage than you could imagine to get into that lift but there were no champagne corks popping or journalists waiting when I got out. Most people use lifts regularly without even thinking about it. But I needed a huge pool of courage, so I'd describe it as one of my proudest moments and it would be up there at the top of my achievements.

Have you:

- run a marathon?
- worked for charity?
- cared for someone?
- overcome a disability, illness or phobia?
- pushed yourself beyond what you thought possible?
- overcome shyness?
- made something?
- had and reared a child?
- won any sport?
- lost weight? (Gaining it doesn't really count!)

These were ideas to get your thinking started – now please carry on!

Personality

In this quadrant you should write words that define or describe your personality, making sure that you use only positives. What is it that's great about you? What personality plus points would you bring with you to a new job? You might find you're now on such a 'high' from compiling the other boxes that you can fill this one three times over. If not, here are some words to get you going:

happy
positive
optimistic
confident
thoughtful
kind
caring
empathetic
determined
honest
trustworthy

shrewd
analytical
thorough
enthusiastic
energetic
focused
keen
hard working
assertive
flexible

Using your Shield

The core job of your Shield is to boost you up and motivate you by making you see yourself in a positive light. But it is also an invaluable tool to help compile your CV as well as marketing yourself during the interview itself.

You now know what you're good at, and all your best points. Once you have your ideal job in mind it's up to you to hone those points, selecting the ones that are of practical value when it comes to applying for and being interviewed for that job. It's a valuable technique to lay the Shield out in front of you and pick out all the best skills, qualifications and competencies for any job you're applying for. Your Shield won't just be an internal confidence-booster, it will also have this direct practical use as a 'pick and mix' of relevant qualities that you can offer to any employer.

Different strokes: how intelligent are you?

I thought you might like to know a couple of fascinating facts about your intelligence levels. Are you bright or brainy? Or do you usually see yourself as 'average' or even 'a bit on the dim side'? There are several different types of intelligence, meaning that although you might be a bit weak, lacking or challenged on one, the chances are you have strengths you might not even have been aware of.

Years ago intelligence was judged via **intelligence quotient** (IQ), with the most intelligent people being the ones who could work out all those written quizzes. But what about all the other parts of the brain?

Dr Howard Gardner, Professor of Education at Harvard University, suggests we have not one but eight possible different intelligences. If you understand these eight options, you can boost your intellectual confidence and present yourself more strongly at interviews.

The Eight Intelligences

- **Linguistic:** you're good with language and can talk well.
- **Logical:** you're good at maths or systems and analysis.
- **Visual/spatial:** you can imagine how things are going to look and you can navigate or draw well.

- **Musical:** you can make music, carry a tune or keep to a beat.
- **Physical:** you can dance, run or play sports.
- **Interpersonal:** you get on well with others.
- **Intrapersonal:** you are self-analytical, understanding your behaviour and your feelings.
- **Naturalist:** (no, not *naturist*!) you live in harmony with the natural world.

All these intelligences are important. Can you see which ones you excel in? Begin to evaluate your own intelligence by more than just your exam results or IQ tests!

IN A NUTSHELL

- See yourself as the product – take an objective and positive look at yourself and your unique selling points.
- Do the Shield activity to form a vital view of your own strengths.
- Evaluate your own intelligence using the Eight Intelligences, not just the normal one! You have value for companies that even you might not be aware of.

3 HOW TO GET AN INTERVIEW

This chapter helps you with practical steps to getting accepted for interview by a company or agency by:

- understanding the three key routes to getting an interview
- looking at the skills of networking or cold-calling
- motivating you to pitch and keep pitching.

Key routes to getting an interview

There are three key routes to getting an interview.

1. **Waiting:** until a job has been advertised and applying for it.
2. **Cold-calling:** applying to a company and asking to be considered for a place, even when one is not currently being advertised as open; or presenting your CV on the Internet. (A 2006 survey by *Personnel Today* found that more than 70% of organisations use online recruitment methods and that percentage is likely to have increased considerably.)
3. **Being headhunted:** networking to make sure you're being seen on the open marketplace or being contacted in your present job by another firm or headhunting agency and asked if you'd be keen to jump ships.

Can I do all three?

Of course! There are no real rules about how to get an interview except this one:

Who dares wins!

If you sit back waiting for your ideal job to come along and whisk you off, you will still be sitting there on that same chair, hoping, for a very long time.

Pitching and marketing yourself is very like marketing any other product. Again, imagine you're a chocolate bar. You look good, taste good and you're ideally priced and smartly packaged. There would be customers out there who would love to buy you. The only problem is they don't know that you exist. Without active marketing to raise your profile all your talent and skills count for nowt.

If you're unemployed, under-used or unhappy in your job you'll have to start out on a campaign to find first-time or alternative employment. This will mean creating written details of all your wonderfulness and abilities (your CV) and then making sure it gets sent to all the right places, along with a covering letter and a back-up telephone call.

Pitching yourself

Are you a natural salesperson? Pitching anything takes nerves of steel and the skin of a rhinoceros. Pitching *yourself* takes nerves of reinforced concrete and the skin of six rhinoceroses placed side by side. Although actually it doesn't. It might *feel* at times as if it does, but all it really needs is the ability to pick up that telephone and ask them to give you a chance.

When you're placing yourself out there on the job market there's little room for either pride or shyness. Paul Jacobs, who has 30 years' experience in the recruitment business, even suggests you should be a bit of a bunny-boiler!

Pitch-perfect

Before we launch into CV and contact planning it would be good for you to sit back and consider one overall piece of advice:

It's not all about you!

Self-obsession is a common theme among jobseekers and a cross-section of the average thoughts of your average applicant would probably be something along the lines of:

- 'I want them to give me this job.'
- 'I deserve some luck.'
- 'I hope they pick me.'

Paul Jacobs advises: 'Brainstorm like stink. Register with agencies but also ask yourself which companies you'd like to work for and approach them directly. Big companies get thousands of applications, which is why they often use an agency, but that's no reason you shouldn't try.

Be bold. Write to the chief executive and explain who you are and why you're applying. Follow it up with a phone call. Your level of belligerence could separate you from the jobseeking masses. You need to put in graft. If it won't come to you, you need to go out to it. Essentials are enthusiasm, energy and a good support system to boost morale. Ask and keep trying because it's easy to start giving up and lose direction if you're not immediately successful.

Treat jobseeking as an experience, like having a career. Campaign. Network with family and friends. In many ways, life's just one big job interview. And watch out about the impression you create in the least obvious places. I know some employers who will use Facebook to check out applicants, watching to see what you put on it and what it tells them about you. Recruiters use it to check your background.'

- 'I will feel better if I get this job.'
- 'I need the money.'
- 'I need the kudos.'
- 'I'd enjoy this career.'
- 'I'd look forward to the challenge.'
- 'I want to feel confident.'
- 'I want to be accepted.'
- 'I want the interviewer to be nice to me and ignore that gap in my employment record where I couldn't be bothered to look for work.'
- 'I want them to skip over the fact I have a bad record for punctuality.'

When you're pitching and making those all-important first approaches to a company it's not what you want that counts – it's what *they* want. It's not as hard as you'd think to slip into the mind of the average interviewer. In many ways, their needs are quite simple:

- 'I want this person's talents and skills to be a perfect fit with the job I'm recruiting for.'
- 'I have to work through a glut of CVs, most from applicants who lack the ability or qualifications to do this job.'
- 'I want to read through CVs that are clear and to the point.'
- 'I want them to be good value, i.e. bringing return for the money we're offering to invest.'
- 'I don't want to wade through a mass of irrelevant detail looking for the right fit.'
- 'I'm not an archaeologist going on a dig, I want the right person to leap out at me.'
- 'I want them to know they're the right person and I need them to know why.'

So, here's a rule to keep at the front of your mind throughout the pitching process:

Put yourself in the interviewer's shoes

A constant reassessment of the whole process seen through their eyes is vital. Or, to strangle a quote from John F. Kennedy: 'Ask not what the company can do for you, ask what you can do for the company'.

How to do your CV

Cyberspace and home printers have opened the borders in recruitment terms. Although this is primarily a good thing (you have access to more vacancies and the ability to post yourself out there where the whole world can see, plus the ability to jet as many copies of your CV across to as many companies as you choose), it has very obvious down sides. The high volume of CVs out there in cyberspace means there is a huge overload and interviewers complain that applicants no longer worry whether they fit the job specifications or not, while many applicants complain that interviewers aren't providing enough job specifications in the first place.

The outcome of this is that most CVs are 'fuzzy' – untailored, non-specific and unsuitable for the position.

This advice should help during the actual interview but also at pitch stage. It will also help explain most of the following dos and don'ts.

DO: make your pitch as wide in scope as you like.

DON'T: make it obvious. Sounding as if a company is just one on a very long list of longshots won't impress anyone. Make all your approaches sound and look personal and specific rather than scattergun.

DO: spend time creating a world-class CV.

DON'T: make it a 'one-size-fits-all' CV. Tailor it for each company you send it to.

DO: update your CV. I recently got one from a guy in his 30s who'd still got details of school achievements in the first paragraph.

DO: make it easy to skim-read. Interviewers are busy people and they don't settle down with a nice hot cup of tea and a pipe full of Old Holborn to read through your CV cover-to-cover. They get loads – possibly sacks full – and they cheat and cut corners like the rest of us. Break your CV down into easily digestible chunks with headlines, like a newspaper.

DON'T: apply the 'Any way to make my CV stand out from all those others just has to be a good idea' theory to CV-making. Personalised touches like blood-red notepaper, 'zany' photos or smiley-face logos *will* make it stand out, but for all the wrong reasons.

DON'T: assume your interviewer/the HR department has a sense of humour.

DON'T: use exclamation marks. (As in 'Hi! I'm Nicola and I'm a media studies graduate with a passion for PR!')

DO: thank the interviewer for reading it in your covering letter.

DON'T: grovel and get too wordy.

DO: create a 'Standout' CV that is easy to read and easy to absorb.

DO: work from the top down. Assume they have a low attention span so stack all your goodies in terms of qualifications and experience at the top of the CV and work downwards. Leaving the best until last might mean the best never gets read at all. This type of CV is called a **reverse chronological CV**.

DO: make sure you've included all the following:

- contact details (believe it or not some candidates miss this off a paper CV)
- qualifications
- skills
- previous employment history (if applicable) including dates
- professional development, i.e. training courses attended
- interests
- referees.

DO: remember that some of your skills will be displayed on your CV itself, such as communication skills, writing skills, attention to detail, neatness and planning. Make sure your own CV doesn't prove you a liar. For instance the claim: 'I have a good eye for detail' will appear pretty stupid if you've written 'I have a good eye fur detail'.

DO: keep using paper CVs as well. You can distribute them at job fairs and use them as an excuse for dropping into a recruitment agency. Paper looks good (please use recycled!) and can be refreshing and pleasant to open, handle and read in a world of online communication. The fact you've bought and gummed a stamp onto an envelope *can* show a level of interest and keenness that online postings fail to do.

Internet recruitment

Sarah El Doori is Marketing Director for Trinity Mirror Digital Recruitment. Her top tips for maximising your chances of finding a job online are:

- 'look for job boards that specialise in the sector that you want to work in. If you don't know where to start, type your key search terms, e.g. 'legal jobs in London' into Google and see which job boards appear on the first two pages
- 'make sure that as well as uploading your CV to a job board, you also make it searchable as recruiters and employers regularly use online CV databases to source and headhunt candidates
- 'most job boards will ask you to create an online profile and you should always complete this, as the more information a recruiter searching a CV database has about a candidate, the greater your chances of being approached,
- 'register for any job alerts or newsletters that the job board offers, as they will use these emails to send you jobs that match your search criteria.'

Always **think laterally** when you decide which companies and sectors to approach. For instance, you could think that the NHS is all about medical staff, but it's not. Doctors and nurses make up less than 40% of the workforce. The NHS is made up of 440 organisations, and their careers website can have details on jobs from hotel services, property and estate work to scientific or health information.

Strategy planning

It's likely you've already reached interview stage but pitching is an ongoing process. You pitch, you interview and you re-pitch if you fail to get that job. Pitching is a campaign that – like your interview techniques – will need re-booting and refreshing regularly if you're going to be successful.

OK, it's roll up your sleeves time. Strategy planning for your pitch should involve all the following steps.

- **Mapping:** selecting the type of job market you're looking in.
- **Snooping:** picking out certain companies you're particularly keen on working for and finding out as much about them as you can (Google is a good start).
- **Matching:** who or what type of person are they looking for? Reading and re-reading any job specification and seeing if your face fits. Or, if there are no vacancies advertised and you're cold-calling, getting a feel for the company

and its culture via the Internet or requested information. Tailoring your CV to ensure you include useful and appropriate details and information.

- **Mating call:** making your pitch by sending or posting your CV, phoning the company, asking for an interview. Or attending recruitment fairs with the aim of getting to interview stage.

How to use a recruitment agency

Paul Jacobs, one of the leading names in recruitment in the UK, advises:
'Whereas in the past most jobseekers would habitually go into a recruitment agency to register and meet a consultant to discuss their next career move, contemporary life has now provided the convenience and ease of going online to register with recruitment consultancies at any time of the day or night.'

A recruitment agency can help pitch you and promote you in the job market rather than taking the direct route between jobseeker and company of employment. There are certain advantages, including access to jobs you might never have known existed, and having someone to promote your talents and skills for you.

A recruitment agency will need you to pitch to them first, and it can be as vital to create a good impression with the agency as it can with a prospective employer, so treat agency interviews in exactly the same way as you would a job interview. Smartness, punctuality, keenness and reliability will all be 'sell-on' qualities than can help push you to the top of the agency books.

Paul Jacobs advises: 'The down side of today's modern instant registration technology is that your CV will automatically be stored on the database of the agency with no human interaction. No conversation with a professional consultant – just silence – and the likelihood is that the agency will not even bother to phone you up, as their volume of applicant registrations means there are just too many CVs for them to search.

'Yours is just another CV hidden in the mass of CVs already cluttering up their expanding database!

'Your CV will be kept on their database, and then when a consultant acquires a new vacancy they will type in keywords and phrases associated with the role to see which CVs emerge that match the search from their extensive database.

'The problem with this process is that it is entirely impersonal. Accurate matching is left to the software of the consultant's computer system.

'Any human intuition and common sense is excluded by this clinical process, and since an individual's personality and attitude have at least as much to do with obtaining a new job as experience or skills, the question is: just how do you get your face known by the recruiter so they understand who you are as an individual, rather than just a random set of competencies outlined on your CV?

'The answer is that you have to be brave enough to get on the phone to them. You need to be belligerent and persistent. Ask if they received your CV and – very important – obtain the name of the person you are dealing with. Attempt to arrange an appointment to see them in person, but if that approach fails just turn up at their offices and ask for the consultant that you spoke to and introduce yourself.

'The opportunity to leave an impression on the consultant who is representing you should not be overlooked or underestimated, it makes the world of difference. Now you are a real-life person to the consultant, not just another CV buried on their computer system.

'Always send a good-quality covering letter with your CV, it will provide you with a chance to stand out from the crowd. Many graduate CVs all look the same, i.e. they'll read something like: 'I'm 22 yrs and have a degree in ...' Your covering letter will express you as a person and help to personalise your application.

'Keep a note of the name of the person your letter goes to, as this can help you get past the receptionist when you call. The receptionist is the 'gatekeeper' and if you can ask for an individual by name, there is a good chance that you will avoid being blocked. It might be pushy, but it can get you on.

'Always look the part. Remember to impress the agency when you go to meet them making the same effort that you would utilise to impress a prospective employer. Never think 'I'm only going to see the agency'. Dress in a business suit, immaculate nails and polished shoes. First impressions count – it's true!

'Try flattery! You could be asked: 'why have you chosen this agency?' Do your research so you can tell them exactly why you selected them, i.e. 'I've come to you because you've been in business for 20 years and have an outstanding reputation, and I have heard fantastic things about you ...'

'It is vital to know exactly what you want in a career and exactly what you don't want to do. Keep an open mind about opportunities, but do not be swayed to take a role that is utterly unsuited to your skill set and personality. You will not enjoy the experience and the chances are that you will not stay long in the job. Not great for your CV!

'Recruitment agencies often have a lot of work in call centres or sales jobs, like selling advertising space. This is fine if it is the kind of work that you would like to do, and you are convinced that you have the ability to succeed, but do avoid being pushed into the wrong job, if you feel uncertain.

'Ask your agency to provide detailed information about the employer they are sending you to meet. They should be well aware of information that you would not readily obtain from your Google or website search, like details of the person you are going to see and what type of questions they are likely to ask you. They could also provide the interviewer with the 'tactile' facts, i.e. useful details about you, for example that you might be nervous or shy during the early stages of the discussion but that you are well qualified for the job.'

IN A NUTSHELL

- Always put yourself in the interviewer's shoes. Jobs aren't given out of kindness. Work out what you can bring to the company and offer that, rather than telling them what the job will mean to you.
- Be professional. Think of jobseeking as a job in itself and plan your strategies carefully, taking on board every route available
- Treat agencies like companies. When you go in to see them, treat it like another job interview.
- Make sure you have the best CV. First impressions count!

4 MENTAL PREPARATION

How to re-boot your confidence

This chapter makes vital reading whether you're attending an interview or even starting a new job because it's all about stages of mental preparation. It helps you through the minefield of shyness, low self-esteem, negativity and lack of confidence by:

- supplying you with a unique set of questionnaires to clarify and diagnose exactly what your 'thinking' problems are and where they stem from.
- taking you through each one of these problems, from stress and anxiety to shyness, and supplying you with tips and techniques to ensure you never allow them to scupper your chances of success again!

Confidence

I've deliberately devoted an entire chapter of this book to the subject of confidence because when I was at research stage – asking people what they would most like to get out of a book on interview techniques – it was the number one request. Number two was the re-motivational skills that can help you cope if the knockbacks become regular and seemingly endless, so there is plenty of advice on that, too.

A large part of your interview success will come under the heading of 'mind over matter' because – in thinking and motivational terms – you won't only be your own worst enemy, you'll be your *only* enemy at interview stage. If you have the right talent, skills and experience the only thing that can scupper your chances will be negativity, anxiety, shyness, stress and lack of confidence.

I've spent many years speaking and writing on the subject of confidence and find it both fascinating and deeply annoying. Why do we get shy? How is it that intellect counts for nothing once the legs start to shake, the hands start to sweat and the mind goes blank?

You might feel like a victim when it comes to confidence, as if you have no power at all when it comes to self-esteem. You might even think that shyness is part of your basic personality and that you can do as little to change it as you can to change the colour of your eyes. But you'd be quite wrong on both counts.

In this chapter you're going to learn how to grow your own confidence to the point where you are able to market yourself effectively and professionally. Some of the advice will take time but most is in the form of quick-hit tips: small steps and changes to your behaviour or thinking that will have a dramatic effect on how you are perceived.

Diagnosing your problem

The first step in containing and controlling any interview anxiety is to make an accurate diagnosis of the problem. Are you suffering from low self-esteem, lack of confidence, shyness or stress? It's important to identify the root cause before you start to deal with the symptoms. What exactly is it about an interview that throws you out of kilter? Understanding your feelings means taking control of them and taking the right steps towards eliminating or at least diminishing them.

Self-esteem

Do your interviews suffer because you have low self-esteem? It's virtually impossible to sell yourself when you have diminished faith in your own potential. You might learn how to mask self-esteem issues and to talk yourself up, but learning how to grow a healthy amount of self-regard will always make your interview experience more enjoyable. A good self-esteem means you'll feel more comfortable about the interview process and more honest answering the questions. It will also help you survive intact if the interview isn't followed up by a job offer. For someone with low self-esteem, a turn-down can seem as a confirmation of your own low expectations. A typical mantra of someone with low self-esteem is: 'I knew that would happen'. This style of thinking can be self-scuppering, as we generally get what we think we deserve. Get working on your self-esteem before you create unnecessary failure!

Is your self-esteem something you've decided upon, or is it what's called a **mirrored self**: a reflection of the comments and opinions of everyone else around you? A mirrored self can be robust, but only if you've always been surrounded by fans, suckers-up and admirers. If you had critical parents, siblings, children or partners and you've allowed their negative opinions to take control of your self-perception you shouldn't be surprised if your self-esteem looks a little like Pete Docherty after a six-week bender.

It's normal to want more confidence when you attend an interview. But did you know your confidence can only be boosted if your self-esteem is in a healthy state? How's your self-esteem? One easy way to evaluate it is to imagine it in terms of a person. How would he or she look? Pallid, weak and runty or robust and blooming?

You have low self-esteem if:

- you find it easier to criticise yourself and list your faults than to talk about your good points
- your opinions are easily swayed
- when you look in a mirror you tend to focus on your 'problem' areas
- when you get low you start to remember all the bad things people have ever said about you
- you were bullied at school and still re-visit those experiences
- you can think of many reasons why the other candidates should get the job you're interviewing for but few if any reasons why it should go to you

- you look to others to praise you and boost you up
- you expect to fail
- you feel uncomfortable with success
- you tend to blame others or situations over which you have no control
- you start to give up if you fail at anything.

ACTIVITY 2

SELF-ESTEEM AUDIT QUESTIONNAIRE

Answer the following questions, then add up your score to check the state of health of your ego:

1. When somebody pays me a compliment I tend to:
   (a) wonder what they're after: why are they buttering me up?
   (b) thank them, feeling very slightly embarrassed
   (c) make a self-effacing comment in reply. If they said they liked my outfit, I'd probably tell them I got it in a sale
   (d) Agree with them and feel self-satisfied as a result.

2. If I pass two people at work who are whispering I tend to assume:
   (a) they're gossiping about someone else: I might even try to join in!
   (b) they're plotting something
   (c) they're discussing something good about my appearance
   (d) they're whispering about me and obviously being critical.

3. When I speak on the phone I tend to:
   (a) use the phrase 'Hi, it's only me'
   (b) use my full name and job title
   (c) ask 'Are you busy or is it a good time to talk?'
   (d) hang up if it's voicemail. I prefer email anyway.

4. You missed out on that promotion. Do you think:
   (a) that's just my luck, I knew I didn't stand a chance
   (b) the person who got it must have slept with the boss
   (c) the person who got it must have more skills or experience. How can I build up my portfolio to ensure I don't miss out next time?
   (d) I can't help getting tongue-tied at interviews.

5. You get stood up on a first date. Do you think:
  (a) he or she must have been involved in a really bad accident
  (b) they probably did turn up but changed their mind and walked away when they saw me
  (c) they're probably too shy. It's easy to bottle things if you lack confidence
  (d) I knew it was too good to be true.

6. When you brought paintings home from school did your parents:
  (a) have them framed and hung on the wall
  (b) ask what they were supposed to be
  (c) stick them on the front of the fridge door with fridge magnets
  (d) tell you you'd never be the next Picasso?

7. Are your friends:
  (a) mainly people you've known all your life – you can relax more with people you know well
  (b) people you enjoy having a good old moan with: a problem shared is a problem halved
  (c) upbeat, optimistic and quite successful in their fields
  (d) often workplace people who can be useful for your career?

8. When an interviewer asks: 'tell me all about yourself' you think:
  (a) how long have you got? You start with your personal details then list all your career achievements to date
  (b) he or she'll only be wanting to hear about my relevant experience. I'll keep it as concise as possible
  (c) I'd better be honest and give a 'warts and all' break-down of my life to date
  (d) I wish they wouldn't ask such difficult questions.

Scores

1. (a) 0; (b) 4; (c) 2; (d) 6
2. (a) 4; (b) 2; (c) 6; (d) 0
3. (a) 0; (b) 6; (c) 4; (d) 2
4. (a) 0; (b) 6; (c) 4; (d) 2
5. (a) 6; (b) 0; (c) 4; (d) 2
6. (a) 6; (b) 0; (c) 4; (d) 2
7. (a) 2; (b) 0; (c) 4; (d) 6
8. (a) 6; (b) 4; (c) 0; (d) 2

Answers

37–48 Your self-esteem is sky-high, possibly even a little too high! There is a risk that you could come across as arrogant, or that you hype yourself up to the point that you forget to evaluate yourself from another person's viewpoint. Do keep up the good work, but do also remember to spot any areas of your CV or interview expertise that you might need to work on.

21–36 Your self-esteem is in pretty good shape, especially if your scores were quite even. You're able to assess yourself in an objective way, recognising the positive as well as any areas that need shoring up. This will give you the ability to survive and thrive at interview level.

11–20 Your self-esteem could do with a little work. You're popular at work but possibly struggle getting your point across or selling your ideas at meetings or interviews. That inner dialogue is telling you that you're less able than you are. Deal with it and become master of yourself. Modesty is good but not as a self-marketing tool.

0–10 Your self-esteem is so low you probably knew you'd do badly in this questionnaire, even before you'd started it. In muscle terms it's currently puny, but like any muscle in the body a bit of gym work and training is probably all that it needs. Devour the tips below and get boosting!

Blame baggage

If you've had a critical upbringing or suffered from bullying at school or belittling from your partner, you'll find it very tempting to blame a cripplingly low self-esteem on them. I once coached a man who had continually failed to shine at internal promotion interviews so that even junior staff were leapfrogging over him to get to management and executive level. His problem was lack of interview confidence, and he blamed this squarely on his childhood. He had a high-achieving older brother and a talented younger sister. In among all this brilliance he found it increasingly difficult to shine. His subsequent naughtiness had been attention seeking (if I can't get your attention by being good I'll get it for being a pain in the arse instead!) and as a result his parents had always been telling him off for being 'stupid'.

Despite having a good career, his **mirrored self** (i.e. low-achieving dimwit) had stuck with him unchallenged throughout his life, popping up at regular intervals when he least needed it, on dates, business presentations and promotion interviews. In many ways he had allowed other people to define his value for him, then dragged that low-value person along for over 30 years. No matter how many times he'd disproved this mirrored self by doing well at university, getting a PhD and proving himself in his job, emotion would outstrip logic and his self-esteem would roll over and play dead every time he was put up for evaluation.

Challenging your mirrored self

If your **mirrored self** is scuppering your potential like this, there are four key tips to help deal with it.

1. **Recognise its existence:** identify its voice of your mirrored self and the sources of its voice.
2. **Challenge yourself:** why do you choose to drag it through life with you?
3. **Challenge its opinion:** give yourself a fresh, objective evaluation based on fact rather than stereotype, unfair comparison or prejudice. On a lighter note, it can help if you deliberately imagine your mirrored-self voice as a stupid-sounding one that diminishes its authority, meaning you can ignore it more easily (high-pitched and whiney works for me!).
4. **Kick its ass:** what happens to you in life – people's opinions, comments, ridicule or insult – forms what's called **stimulus**. Although you may have no ability to control this stimulus (most of it will be comments from the past anyway!), you do have the option of controlling your **response** to that stimulus. Why allow other people to control your feelings, your self-esteem and – ultimately – your life? Didn't they do enough damage with their words? Why choose to take those words with you in your head and agree with them when the going gets tough? When you can't change the stimulus, look to change the response. Stop allowing other people to have a negative effect on your own self-esteem.

You're not alone in your mirrored-self issues. Ego is an oddly fickle little thing and one thing I have discovered from my years of working in business is that there are very few people (and I'm including chief execs and captains of industry) who aren't sitting at their desks waiting to be sussed as a complete waste of space at any given time.

I always remember one tall blonde woman working on a TV series (OK, it was me!) who was bursting with confidence, right up to the moment the producer pulled her off a rehearsal and asked to have a chat. In that 10-second walk to the office it occurred to me in a blinding flash that they'd finally realised I was utter pants, in fact pants-vest-and-socks, and were about to bounce me off the show. To my utter shame I even let this deluge of negativity show in my body language. Happily it turned out someone else was for the chop and they wanted me to take over their slot too! But I've never forgotten how quickly, dramatically and totally I morphed from hero to zero. It was as if my ego waved goodbye to my body with a 'you're on your own from here'.

How to boost self-esteem in six easy steps

Psychologist Arnold Buss defines the six main sources of self-esteem.

1. **Appearance:** feeling you look attractive makes you feel better about yourself.
2. **Ability and performance:** achievement and good grades will boost your ego.
3. **Power:** being in control of your destiny and your life.
4. **Social rewards:** getting praise, affection and respect from other people.
5. **Vicarious:** things like reflected glory, having important colleagues or powerful, popular friends.
6. **Morality:** being a good person and holding sound values.

How does this help you during the interview process? Well, if you can understand exactly what motivates and massages your self-esteem, it's relatively easy to start work on inflating it with a foot pump. OK, so you won't undo years of damage caused by that bigger kid who used to call you 'numb-nuts' in the playground, but you can still get some emergency work in before that interview.

Appearance

Working on your appearance is something you'll be doing anyway, but it's interesting to note that your smart, well-pressed suit, well-cut hair and gleaming nails aren't only done to impress the interview panel. They have a very strong effect on your self-perception and sense of worth too, so get ironing!

Ability

Next, you need to take stock of both your Shield and your CV. On them, you'll have listed all your achievements, experience, good points and qualifications. You know your Shield was compiled to boost your self-esteem but – like your business suit – you probably think your CV has been written exclusively for external marketing. In reality, it has a dual roles as you can read it through and marvel at all your wonderful skills and qualities just before you go into the interview room.

Power

You might think that power is a trickier issue. However, power is by and large perceptual and you can achieve a quick fix in a matter of moments by changing the script in your head. Instead of thinking things like 'I *have* to get up early for the interview' ... 'I *have* to show up on time' ... 'I *have* to make a good impression', substitute the word 'choose' for the word 'have', i.e. 'I *choose* to arrive on time', and so on. This will give you a much more profound feeling of being in control of your world, your destiny and your environment.

Social rewards

This is where we can return to the mirrored self. You *could* go around trying to gather up compliments from all and sundry before your interview. However, this is one form of self-esteem boosting that you might like to question before an interview. Good reviews and flattery from other people will be of less use on this occasion than self-coaching, i.e. talking yourself up *to* yourself. Try telling *yourself* how good you are rather than asking others.

Vicarious

Name dropping might sound gross but do it well and you could boost your interview profile as well as your self-esteem. OK, so your conversation shouldn't be littered with name-drops but it won't hurt to use some associations, as long as you're relatively subtle about it. Have you worked for any known business people? Have you ever met anyone who might be counted as impressive? Did you ever go to a lecture by a leading sports personality or get trained by someone with a good reputation?

Morality

Some quiet moments reflecting on or even listing all your values will help boost your confidence. Widen the scope of your self-esteem by reminding yourself of all the occasions you've been helpful, principled, honourable and decent, even if you never got any praise for it. Do you recycle or work to help the environment? Are you a carer or do you do any work for charity? Reminding yourself that you're an honourable human being can be a wonderful puff just before an interview.

Coping with confidence

Confidence sits on top of your self-esteem, but whereas self-esteem can appear to be 'fixed', your confidence levels probably fluctuate depending on the occasion or who you are dealing with. *Over*-confidence can be vile and destructive if it creates the kind of arrogance that prevents you from preparing and working hard to excel, but *good* confidence is the type that allows you to think and communicate in a way that markets you in a positive light.

What is confidence? The first three letters of the word are very telling! Confidence is a bit of a con-trick. Most people lack it but some are just better at hiding their shyness and lack of self-assurance than others. For life's great performance moments, like a job interview, your confidence levels need to be measured on a sliding scale. How nervous/anxious/stomach-churningly stressed do you get?

Rate yourself on a scale of 1–10 with '1' being laid back and pretty relaxed and '10' being 'I could gnaw my own fingernails to stumps and then have my toenails as dessert'.

If you said '11', you're in good company, although you might also have said that it depends on who's interviewing you for what job and how much is at stake. Some interviewers will go to great pains to help you relax because they realise it's the best way to get honest information out of you. Others are clearly fans of the old 'SAS Interrogation Techniques' manual. The good news is it matters not, as the following pages are going to contain good solid advice to enable you to overcome stress and nerves and get through any interview with the maximum confidence.

You lack confidence if:

- you hate the idea of standing in a room full of strangers at an interview or interview presentation

- you tend to warm up as you go along – it's the idea of people you don't know that makes you nervous
- you tend to stammer or get tongue-tied at interviews
- you're happy to get an interview over as quickly as possible, even if you don't have enough time to make all your points
- you have trouble making eye contact with the interviewer
- verbally you either clam up or waffle too much
- you often hear yourself saying the wrong thing but seem powerless to shut yourself up
- you often forget to smile
- your handshake is often clammy
- you get clumsy during the interview
- you know you're good at your job but you have difficulty putting that message across.

The confidence triangle

This is a nice, simple blueprint for the way your mind produces confidence or lack of it.

The confidence triangle

- **Stage 1:** you have a thought in your head. You have an interview coming up. Your thought is – let's say – 'I'm never any good at interviews'.
- **Stage 2:** that thought gets translated into your feelings. Already you can see how a thought like that is going to pan out in terms of feelings of

confidence. If you're telling yourself you're no good, then you're likely to begin suffering from a degree of nervousness and anxiety. This is where your survival system kicks in. Your survival process is stunningly simplistic. If it starts to feel anxiety building up, it assumes you're being chased by a bear or a sabre-toothed lion or some prehistoric equivalent. You'll read exactly where all this fight–flight stuff goes to in the section on stress but for the time being let's agree that you're going to start to get the jitters.

- **Stage 3:** although very mild anxiety or nerves can produce sterling performances anywhere, from a job interview to the stage at the O_2 arena, the jitters are likely to cause problems. Once they've scuppered your performance or interview, your original thought of 'I'm never any good at interviews' will appear to have had some serious endorsement, making it even tougher to challenge. And so the whole process begins again – only with each run around the triangle things get worse and worse and worse ...

I know about the jitters because I've been there myself very recently. Lured by the idea 'it will be a laugh' I agreed to be a contestant on *Celebrity Weakest Link*. If you don't know the programme, it involves answering general knowledge questions and being insulted wholesale by Anne Robinson. Although I never get seriously nervous on TV, I realised as I faced Anne that incontinence knickers might have been a good idea. The effect of this fear on my intellectual skills was phenomenal. It took all my knowledge and experience of confidence-coaching and brain-training to answer even simple questions like: 'what's your name?' and 'what do you do?' The fact I didn't go out in Round 1 is testimony to the fact that the tips I'm about to give you work!

Instant confidence boosters

Break the chain of **think – feel – behave** by making changes at any point of the triangle. Change your thought. Challenge your feelings. Change your behaviour or 'state'.

The quickest way to change your thoughts is by creating positive affirmations. Make up a few upbeat mantras to yourself and keep repeating them. Try:

- I love interviews
- I know I can do well
- I'm good at this sort of thing
- I feel calm, confident and in control.

Sounds too easy? Then there's no reason not to try it, is there? These messages will start to bypass your conscious mind if you keep repeating them enough. Otherwise you'll just be bombarding your subconscious with messages like 'I'm dreading this', which will cause increased anxiety.

These new thoughts should impact on your feelings but you can throw some exercises into the mix for good measure. Breathe in gently, hold it for one second and then breathe out loads. Empty your lungs. And empty all your anxiety out along with all that old, expelled air.

Or you can change your behaviour by changing your state. By this, I mean change the way you look. Your body language isn't all about external projection, a lot of the time it's sending a lot of internal perception signals that can increase any lack of confidence. Pull yourself up to full height and smile. Then laugh. Then laugh at yourself laughing. (**Note:** Do none of these last two things in front of your interviewer. He or she will think you're more in need of an exorcist than a job offer!)

I train Olympic coaches and *they* train their teams to manage any lack of confidence by telling them this:

When you get butterflies in your stomach don't try to get rid of them, get them flying in formation instead

Don't struggle trying not to be nervous, it's a natural emotion at something like an interview. Instead, harness your nerves to make your performance better. Adrenalin is a wonderful thing if you can get in under control!

Pretend to be someone else. This is great. You'll be attending your interview as *you*, but that doesn't mean to say you can't get a little help by mental role-playing as well. Who do you know who is brave and full of confidence? Who can you think of that would laugh in the face of an interview and be totally unfazed by the thought of answering some killer questions? Pick your character, then adopt some of their chutzpah. I borrow from Emma Peel from *The Avengers* all the time. You might prefer Bear Grylls or Superman, it's up to you. (**Note:** Please take this role-play no further than a quick loan of your character's bravery. No fancy dress please, it's not *Stars in their Eyes*.)

Dealing with shyness

Are you shy? Or do you suffer from intermittent shyness?

Shyness might sound like a childlike response but it can affect adults throughout their lives. Many of those adults will hold down top jobs that involve constant interaction with other people. Strange! Shyness is common in high-profile performance professions like acting and it's not uncommon to meet a leading actor who can give his or her all on stage but be unable to look people in the eye or even speak fluently when at a social event. Social shyness can be annoying and uncomfortable but shyness at an interview can be much more serious. Some levels of interview shyness can be natural but if your shyness means you're unable to communicate effectively it will need to go!

Shyness is a natural animal response of fear in the face of other animals that are a stranger to it. In the animal kingdom that fear can be a life-saver but at a job interview you're unlikely to meet with an interviewer who has the intention of ripping your gullet out with his or her bare teeth.

Having suffered from shyness most of my life, I believe it to be a state of vanity in adults. It's the assumption that everyone has noticed you that is revealing. A shy person will walk into a party and suffer because *'everyone's looking at me'*. But are they? Why should you stand out so much? I learned very quickly that other people notice us a whole lot less than we think. In fact – perversely – it's often the shy person who is dressed or acting in a way to attract attention in the first place. Or they choose a profession that requires them to take to the stage or perform in front of cameras.

You know you're shy if:

- your friends describe you as 'quiet'
- you often want to speak up but tend to over-analyse any response to your words first and then decide to keep quiet
- you often feel like Alice in Wonderland at social events, after she'd grown taller and bigger!
- there are people you've met and wanted to speak to or people you've been attracted to and wanted to engage in conversation but you've held back
- you tend to allow your partner/mother/friend to do all the speaking for you

- conversation with strangers tends to dry up after a couple of questions or statements
- you'd love to be invisible so you could enjoy yourself without having to interact.

The good news is that shyness is an option, not a given. As behaviours go, it's one of the easiest ones to change. How? The answer's simple:

Stop *acting* shy!

I know because I did it. I still feel shy but I no longer look shy or speak shy. Shyness can be treated like indigestion: know when you're getting it and take steps to make it go away.

Shyness behaviour and thinking is a little like a costume or garment: you can choose to wear it today or you can choose not to. We all learn patterns of responses to stimulus from the day we're born and shyness, with its 'stop moving, stop talking and do nothing apart from blush' response probably held you in good stead at some time or another.

Shyness can even produce symptoms that make you more attractive to members of the opposite sex, with all that head-dipping, nervous smiling, eyelash-fluttering and averted eye-gaze. Some shy people do look adorable and female celebs will often adopt the visual symptoms of shyness just to add to their attraction value (Paris Hilton, Carla Bruni, Naomi Campbell, Madonna and Claudia Schiffer are just a few names that come to mind with the 'fake it to make it' attitude to shyness displays).

If you analyse these symptoms, you'll see they do you not one whit of good at a job interview. Cuteness, whimsy, diffidence, going quiet, keeping still ... would you really recommend anyone uses them as a tactic to kick-start a brilliant career?

Tips to deal with your shyness

Stop telling people you're shy. When you tell other people, you tell yourself too. If you're going to change your self-perception this is a vital first step.

Visualise yourself being shy at an interview. Forget your feelings, just go for the performance. What do you do? How do you look? How do you sound?

These are the symptoms you need to address. Feeling shy but not looking or sounding shy is a good goal to be starting with.

Now visualise yourself being un-shy. You ooze charisma and an ability to communicate readily and easily. You want to talk and you want to be heard. How does this 'you' look? What is it doing? What is it saying? Keep looking and keep learning. This is the 'you' you'll be taking to that interview.

Create some un-shy body language (see Chapter 6) and also some un-shy lines of speech. This might sound like visual and verbal scripting, but I promise you that knowing how to sit and having a couple of good lines in your head to break the ice with will put you at a huge advantage.

Imagine your interviewer is shy, too. Top people can feel just as shy as you do, it's just that they're often better at masking the symptoms.

Make statements beginning with 'I', as in 'I'm so pleased to have this opportunity of meeting you/being considered for the job' or 'I enjoyed the journey/cup of coffee/challenge'. These are active statements. Shy people tend to use passive statements that only emerge in reply to questions, such as:

- **Interviewer:** Did you have a good journey?
- **Shy candidate:** Yes thanks

Managing stress

Stress is a very 'popular' problem; many people self-diagnose themselves as suffering from it although very few people really understand what it is. Stress is related to fear, anxiety and panic but fear doesn't have to result in stress.

If you're temporarily sleepless or anxious about an interview it's unlikely that this is stress. But if the problem is recurring and affecting other parts of your life, it could be time to do a brief stress audit.

In many ways, stress is a perfectly natural and desirable response to problems. It's part of your fight–flight mechanism and can be a life-saver if you're under threat or attack. Stress can affect you in three ways.

1. **Physically:** symptoms that range from headaches, indigestion, palpitations and sweating to heart problems and a disruption of the immune system.
2. **Intellectually:** making concentration difficult.
3. **Emotionally:** creating irritability, tears and a feeling of dread.

So far, so bad!

Now the good news: If you were in a bit of a spot, i.e. trapped by a man-eating lion, your stress response would make you faster and stronger. Your breathing would become shallow and more frequent, your pulse would quicken, your skin would sweat, your muscles would tense, your digestive system would take a break and your bowel and bladder would start to empty. All good in the case of the lion because you've become a lean, mean fighting (or running) machine. In the case of a job interview, some of these life-saving symptoms become less than desirable. Hyperventilation, palpitations, sweaty handshakes, lockjaw, giddiness, indigestion and a desire to get to a toilet sooner rather than later aren't the best of party pieces to help secure that ideal job or promotion!

Stress sounds debilitating and so it is. How can you tackle it on the run-up to an interview?

Unlike mild anxiety or fear that can be prompted by the idea of an interview, stress tends to be a habitual response that will probably have built up over time and linked to causes and triggers that have nothing to do with your interview. In many ways, stress build-up is like baggage that we accrue with every difficult situation we go through. Although it usually begins over a big life issue, the stress-response triggers can get smaller and smaller with time, until you feel it's possible to get wound up over virtually nothing.

We don't all get stressed over the same things. You might go through a very challenging or traumatic event in your life with comparative ease, then stress out over a lost mobile phone or buying someone a birthday present. We all have our own individual level of over-stress. Some people love drama in their lives; others prefer a quiet life. Some people thrive on pressure; others buckle under it. There is absolutely no reason to assume your interview will make you stressed, so don't be a stress hypochondriac! If you do begin to become over-stressed, you need to start tackling the problem as early as possible.

Stress is complex, then, but the 'cure' is relatively simple. Stress is caused by mind over matter, i.e. your brain sending the wrong signals down to your body. You're looking at something that isn't life-threatening, like your interview, and telling your body that it is, making it go on full alert.

You're probably stressed if:

- you get insomnia regularly the night before an interview
- you often get physical symptoms, like a headache, shaking hands, palpitations or dizziness
- you get tearful or irritable before an interview
- you tend to dry altogether during interviews – sometimes you can't even hear the questions properly
- you forget easy facts about yourself, like the names of previous employers
- you experience feelings of doom about the interview
- you allow bizarre events to make you late for an interview, like dithering over your choice of outfit, losing your car keys or rushing back because you think you've left the toaster on.

Managing your stress levels

You need to heal from source, meaning you need to start challenging your perceptions. Your interview isn't threatening. It's not a man-eating lion. It's challenging, daunting, exciting, nerve-wracking, annoying, boring, important, desperately important, any or all of the above, but you're not going to lose either your life or a limb attending it. Remind yourself of that. Repeat, repeat, repeat: 'it's not a lion'.

Create a **leader voice** in your head to control your thoughts. Write down the messages you want to hear on the day of the interview and get your leader voice to repeat them to you.

Create a **Little Book of Madness** on the build-up to your interview. This is a notebook that you keep with you to scribble down all your negative or fearful thoughts. Keep it by your bedside at night and write down what's flooding your head if you find you can't sleep. You can even take it to the interview with you to keep writing in right until you go into the company. This helps achieve what psychologists call 'closure'. Your brain will feel that it has dealt with the problem by off-loading the emotional build-up.

Find ways of reminding yourself that there are other, more important things in life. Your mind is getting things out of proportion. An interview is important but not important enough be producing these negative feelings. This is just a moment in your life, not your life.

Call the interview or the interviewers a funny name in your head. Make it a silly name, not a fearful, negative name. Place something fun and silly next to or in front of your alarm clock before you go to sleep.

Watch something lighthearted and fun before you go to bed the night before the interview. The last thing you see or read will affect the nature of your dreams and your sleep. Avoid business books or anything too heavy or depressing. A cartoon or favourite comedy will help put you in the right frame of mind.

Busting failure addiction

Failure addiction? Yes, it's more common than you might think. The problem with failure is that it can begin to feel comfortable because it feels familiar. If your past has been littered with moments that you have labelled as being 'failures' you might be subconsciously moving towards that state again. The lure of familiarity should never be underestimated. Often it's the easy option and what feels like the safest option, even if our conscious mind strives for and yearns for success.

Success sounds great, but it can make people fearful. This is called **The Tall Poppy Syndrome** and I have written a book about it already. It's a strange but common self-scuppering process, where a deep-rooted fear of change or challenge caused by success can lead to us ensuring that it doesn't happen.

The formula can go something like this.

- **What happens if I succeed?** Start new job with consequential new and unknown challenges ... Massive life-change ... New responsibilities that could be stressful ... Alienation of friends and family due to those new responsibilities.
- **What happens if I fail?** I get upset and people are nice to me ... Comfort and encouragement from friends and family ... No change in my current circumstances ... Keeping with what I know.

I know neither of these circumstances is a given but your subconscious mind might believe them.

You know you're addicted to failure if:

- you wake up worrying about what you'll do if you **are** offered the job
- preparing for the interview makes your anxiety increase: better to play it by ear and see what happens
- you take no steps to change what you're doing, even if you get no offers from your first batch of interviews
- you're happy to blame others for any lack of success
- you refuse to imagine yourself getting the job or promotion because it will only make things more painful
- you prefer to set your expectations low, so any success will be a nice surprise
- you mean to do research on the company or study for potential questions but something always goes wrong, like they don't post you through the company handbook you requested or your PC refuses to go online at the last minute
- you always tend to get sick or become 'accident prone' when you've got an interview to go to
- you only pay sketchy attention to planning your journey, often arriving late
- you tend to arrive with your fingers crossed, hoping they won't ask about that gap in your CV
- you have no idea what your body language does during an interview: better to not know than to become uncomfortable and self-aware
- you think they'll like you for your sense of humour
- you believe the friends who've told you to lie about your hobbies and interests
- you've been for a quick drink first to calm your nerves.

Be honest – does any of this sound familiar?

ACTIVITY 2

DEAL WITH FAILURE ADDICTION

Write a list of all the positive things that might happen if you succeed.

Write another list of all the reasons why you *deserve* to be successful.

Draw a large circle on a piece of paper, then draw a small picture of yourself inside that circle. This is you inside your bubble of comfort. Analyse how it feels to be in there, including thoughts like 'safe', 'bored', 'happy' or 'depressed'.

Now draw a larger circle above the first one. This is your success bubble. To get to it you'll need to go through a degree of discomfort, but that's all the feelings change will create, just mild discomfort. Once you're there in your new job and you know what you're doing you will be in this new bubble of comfort, which is miles above the first one, but still – eventually – comfortable. Once you've got there you can move up to the next bubble. The point is, you keep moving upward and any discomfort goes away as you stretch and grow.

Ban yourself from using dialogues that are preparing you to fail, like: 'I know everyone else at the interview will be better qualified/more experienced than I am.' Every time a negative-expectation thought like that pops into your head, bin it and create a new, positive one instead.

Avoid sharing your gloom with friends and family in the hope they'll cheer you up or talk you out of it. Negative thinking is like cling-film – it stretches to cover the widest area. You'll probably end up depressing them as well!

Finally, you're going to be posting these vital messages to yourself.

- **No sick notes!** If you've been creating a mental list of feeble excuses why you're going to fail, then delete it straight away! Excuses are for lily-livered surrender-monkeys! Have a word with yourself, as we say in this part of North London!

- **No whingeing!** Did you ever hear the mantra that the Royal Family are supposed to use in the face of criticism and adversity? It's '*Never complain, never explain!*' At least have a crack at the first part!
- **Moaning is tiresome and contagious.** It might feel therapeutic but I promise you it's not, especially not if it's done on a serial basis. Did you ever fall over in the playground and scrape your knee? Did it scab? What did your mum tell you not to do with that scab? 'Don't pick it because it won't heal.' Moaning is like picking a scab, it just stops you healing and moving on.

IN A NUTSHELL

- Challenge your 'mirrored' self: why be the product of other peoples' perceptions?
- Work on things like your appearance, ability and power.
- Change one corner of your confidence triangle.
- Create your **leader voice** to control your thinking in difficult situations.
- Talk yourself up using **positive affirmations**.
- No sick notes and no whingeing!
- Get your butterflies flying in formation!

5 COPING WITH REJECTION

Already? Before I've been on my first interview! Won't I be guilty of negative thinking?

The fact is that now is the best time to be building up your rejection immune system as it will mean that, although you'll be celebrating an interview success if you get a job offer, a turn-down won't send you into a backward spiral either. This chapter is all about strengthening your self-motivation skills by:

- taking the power over your emotions and responses back into your own hands
- learning how to 'shrug' rather than crumple in the face of any rejection
- avoiding unhelpful responses like denial or blaming others
- investigating what really went wrong
- planning change to ensure success next time.

No pain no gain!

It's a sad fact of life that not everyone thinks we're as brimming with wonderfulness as *we* do, and that not every job that's advertised is tailor-made for our talents or skills. As you probably know by now – especially if you've already started your job search or are on a second or third job – rejection does tend to be part of the recruitment process. Not a *nice* part – masochists only need apply! – but as the saying goes:

That which doesn't kill me makes me stronger

(Although the creator of this maxim had clearly never sampled my cooking!)

This means you are going to have to learn to cope with potential (and possibly serial) rejection. Rejection sorts out the mice from the men: you either come to grips with it and use it as a tool for improvement or you give up and start sucking your thumb. Recycling rejection – i.e. parrying the bruising of your ego while learning how to pick over the bones of the more logical and fruitful part of the experience – is the route we're taking in this book. By taking it under the chin emotionally you take control of your own fate, rather than allowing yourself to be de-motivated, de-energised or even unravelled in terms of confidence and self-esteem.

Stimulus and response

Let's knock that knock-back into context. Always remember that what happens to you is only stimulus. Even if you can't control the **stimulus** – i.e. you miss out one or more jobs – you can always put your energies and efforts into taking control of your **response**. Whether it feels like it or not, it is up to you how you respond to events like rejection. No one else should have sufficient control over you life to make you scupper your next set of interviews by negative or unhelpful thinking and behaviour. When you stop making an effort or start getting scared of your next interview you've allowed a previous interviewer or interview experience to take too much control over your life. Start to shrug it off!

How to shrug

Shrugging off rejection is a useful talent, but one quick word of warning before we discover how to do it.

Don't over-shrug!

What's over-shrugging? Well we've all watched those contestants on reality talent shows who shrug off rejection by exiting yelling: 'you'll be sorry, I'll be back and I'll show you!' to the judges while the great British public yells collectively at its TV screens: 'no you won't, you're rubbish!' Misplaced over-confidence or arrogance can be as self-defeating as low self-esteem, especially if they come welded to a complete and utter lack of talent or potential. (This is why all the claims you will be making about *your* talents and skills on your CV or during your interview itself will be backed up by proof.) Watching the candidates on programmes like *The Apprentice* with their hyped claims like: 'I'm the best salesman in the country' or 'I only deal in success, I can't spell the 'f' word (failure) and I refuse to recognise it' makes for amusing TV as they tumble out of the show in quick succession. There should be an important lesson for you, in all this orgy of hubris, about your own levels of confidence, as opposed to empty arrogance. Over-inflated self-esteem or arrogance leads to rejection-denial, meaning you won't make any effort to change or improve. It is vital that your efforts to shore up your bruised ego don't include failing to take an objective view of your efforts in a bid to do better next time!

Making shrugging work

We've also seen the likes of pop star Darius Danesh, who was rejected by the TV talent judges first time around, but who went away and learned and improved and returned to achieve high levels of success. Darius does have genuine talent, so his self-aggrandising claims about having a number one single despite being turned down were not based on wildly unfounded aspirations. The boy could sing and he made his return in a second reality show and proved it to the entire nation, having employed earlier criticisms to help change his image and his approach – rather than sitting in his bedroom sobbing uncontrollably and sulking for the next year or so.

Rejection teaches you one of two lessons: either you can believe you should give up because you're not good enough, or you can find out what went wrong and learn how to improve or learn to try somewhere else.

The problem is that any rejection can deal what feels like a body blow to your self-esteem. But you do need to remember this: the interviewers weren't rejecting *you*, they were just turning you down for this job.

How rejection works from the interviewer's side

Ever wondered exactly how the rejection process works? The peek-behind-the-scenes example I always use is of a casting I was involved with to find a male presenter to work with me for a training video I was shooting. I was one of a panel doing the interviewing but I was also the prime decision-taker.

We saw 20 men.

- Of those 20 not one was rejected for being rubbish.
- One wasn't selected because he was *too* good-looking.
- One had a face that was too well-known on TV.
- One was too good and had to work with me (not too good!).

Were those three ever informed about the reason for their rejection? Not at first – although I did remember to let them know once I had gone into 'empathy mode' rather than 'interviewer mode'. So what do you think Mr 'too well-known' must have thought at first about being rejected for a diddly job like a training video? What would have been going through his mind? Compare his thoughts to any you might have had following a rejection. Getting turned down for a low-grade or even silly job is more soul destroying than getting rejected for a big one. It's a bit like Madonna might feel if John McCririck turned her down for a date. I'm sure that wonderful, famous and totally over-qualified actor would have been secretly devastated. The point is that any of those talented rejections might have felt the same. The big point for you to learn is that they weren't rubbish, far from it. These guys were about as far away from rubbish as McCririck is from Brad Pitt.

Those guys were good – and so are you. They all had strengths, talents and abilities but all came in different packages. They just weren't right for *that* job. Keep that thought in your mind. Even if you're not going on theatrical castings, the sentiment is the same.

After any interview you should:

- assess your performance
- re-visit your qualifications: did they match the job?

- re-visit your level of experience: was there anything they wanted that I have no experience of?
- ask the company for feedback.

Once you've done all these things you can start to re-boot your confidence and self-esteem. You do this by understanding how your brain works to control your emotions.

Defence mechanisms

Your brain will probably cope with the discomfort of rejection the illogical way, without you ever being aware what's happening. This is Freud's theory of **Defence Mechanisms** (and that's Sigmund, not Clement!).

Freud? In a book about interview techniques? Well yes, actually, and let me explain why. Rejection of any kind can produce some rather odd responses, some of which can be detrimental to moving forward in a positive way towards your next batch of interviews. Freud defined what he called Defence Mechanisms, and most applied to trauma. However, a job rejection can feel like a mini-trauma, so it's valuable to understand how your brain might decide to deal with it. The mind is very good at protecting your ego. To do this it will sometimes go to great lengths to save it from and attack or to repair it when an attack has occurred. In this case the ego-attack is the fact that you have offered yourself to a company and they have decided to turn you down. This ego-protection can take many forms but the ones I most want you to think about are given below.

- **Repression:** keeping that rejection out of your conscious thinking, i.e. trying to ignore it.
- **Denial:** refusing to accept the fact that you were rejected.
- **Rationalisation:** creating an excuse that is more acceptable to your ego but totally incorrect.
- **Regression:** behaving childishly in response to rejection.

Do any of these sound remotely familiar? Have you ever coped with a recruitment rejection with any of the following statements.

- 'They knew who they wanted all along.'
- 'I don't believe there was ever a job there – I think they were just going through the motions.'
- 'I could tell they didn't like me the moment I walked in.'
- 'The interviewer took against me because I'm more attractive and she felt threatened.'
- 'They can stuff their job.'
- 'I wouldn't have taken it if they had offered it to me.'
- 'I could tell they felt threatened by me, I clearly know more about the job than the interviewer did.'
- 'I think my old boss must have got in touch somehow and scuppered my chances. I know the references were OK, but I wonder if he's had a quiet word over a game of golf or something?'
- 'I knew I shouldn't have worn that tie my wife picked out.'
- 'I'm never – ever – going on another interview as long as I live!

Discover the truth

Although it is essential to keep your self-esteem, confidence and ego intact throughout the interview process, even if that means sitting down every night with a jar of glue and a huge roll of sticky tape, it is also essential that you are able to evaluate your interview 'performance' as objectively as possible.

If you are going to go down the route of Freud's Defence Mechanisms you could find you are making yourself oblivious to things that should be changed. For instance, how would a state of denial help if you kept getting knocked back by dates because you had personal hygiene problems? Should you:

- ignore what you're told and carry on *sans* deodorant – after all, there are plenty more fish in the sea?
- get a bath, get some antiperspirant and get going again?

So it's good to take steps to buffer your self-esteem in the face of any rejections. But it's bad to buffer to the point where you're unable to evaluate and make changes accordingly.

If you are rejected by one company, it is a very useful discipline to sit yourself down with a large sheet of paper and ask yourself the question:

What went wrong?

Was it the interview ...?

- What was said?
- What was asked?
- How did I respond?
- How did I feel?
- How did the interviewer appear to respond to my answers?
- Were there any moments where I felt my performance dipped?
- Were there any questions that I felt I could have handled better?

... or was it me?

- How did I look?
- Was my outfit smart enough?
- Did I appear to fit in with my surroundings?
- Did I arrive on time?
- Did I arrive looking relaxed and confident?
- Were my greetings good?
- Did I shake hands well and remember the interviewers' names?
- Did I remember to listen more than I talked?
- Did I use eye contact?
- Did I remember to smile?
- How did I sit in the chair?
- Was my etiquette good?
- Did I speak clearly and concisely?
- Was I able to make myself understood?
- Did I know the answers to all the questions?
- Did I start lying or bluffing?
- Did I look terrified or keen?
- Did I 'fit' the job I was going for?
- Did I thank them for seeing me?
- Were there any questions I felt weak on?
- Could my answers have been better?
- What have I learned from this interview?

It is a useful discipline to spend a while in the interviewer's shoes. Instead of considering that interview from your perspective, try to imagine it through the interviewer's eyes. How did you look to them? Imagine someone has no pre-conceived ideas about you at all, how would they assess you during the space of that interview process?

Removing all emotions from a rejection is hard but vital. Remember, the only view worth assessing is an objective one. Bitterness, anger, paranoia, frustration and misery all need removing from the arena, because they'll make your assessment biased. Bin them. Go and punch a pillow first if it helps but then set about your analysis without them in your head.

How can I improve?

Once you have some answers, go on to your next key question which is: 'how can I make sure that doesn't happen again?'. Positive tactics mean you will learn from a rejection, but only if you can answer this question honestly and without prejudice.

Move and improve. Be strategic, not silly.

It could be that you will genuinely conclude that there is nothing you should or could change before your next interview. If so, stand down. But if you do feel that you were weak on one or two questions or vulnerable on a couple of points or could have worked on your delivery or confidence, do it!

Ask an expert

You don't just have to sit gazing at your own navel in a bid to find out what went wrong. There are other opinions to be gleaned. Just make sure you pick your experts wisely. Who do you think knows the real reasons why you were rejected for a job?

- You.
- The company or interviewer who rejected you.
- Someone you know who has had a good amount of interview success, who is an expert on communications and who writes books like this.
- Your mates.
- Your mum and dad.
- The taxi driver.
- That bloke in the supermarket queue.

The first three are the only real experts when it comes to getting valuable feedback and opinion. So why do so many of us listen to the opinions of rank amateurs? Because they say what we *want* to hear rather than what we *should* hear, that's why! Stay away from the faux experts, the people who suddenly pretend to be the font of all wisdom. If you're young, please understand that being old doesn't automatically make someone an authority. When I was 10 I thought girls of 12½ must know everything there is to know about sex and life in general, just because they were older than me. Forget the sex experts, we clustered around the milk monitor from the next class up just to hear all about how babies come out of your navel!

Just because your uncle, neighbour or partner has an opinion doesn't make him or her an expert. Did they achieve greatness at interview level themselves? And even if they did, there's a world of difference in doing well and being analytical enough to coach someone else into doing well too.

The good news is, you already have access to two experts – yourself and this book. The other piece of excellent news is that there is nothing preventing you from asking the interviewing company the reasons why you didn't get a job offer.

The only slightly less good news is that their feedback might not be entirely honest. They're likely to be very careful about what they tell you and how they tell it. They may have seen hundreds of applicants, although they should have kept thorough notes on each one. Interviewer feedback can be a little like a school report. But it's still very valuable. It might be a total surprise to you, going completely against your own speculation and therefore prevent you barking up the wrong tree. Or it might just confirm what you already guessed. Either way, there is more detailed advice about asking for feedback below.

How to recycle rejection

Do you recycle papers at work or household waste? Recycling any job rejection can be done in exactly the same way. Once you have garnered as much information as possible about why you might not have been given an offer, you need to decide exactly what to do with that information. Is it of use? Or does it need a 'no action necessary' sticker applied to it? You're going to take all the thoughts and feedback and allot it to its right place in your recycling 'bins'.

Bin it: bin any comments that you have either no ability or no desire to change. You could have had a very bad interviewer who has based his or her judgement on an unfair evaluation. Or you could have found you lacked a qualification or skill that you have no ability to acquire. They might have been seeking a higher or lower level of experience and you have no option about achieving that before your next interview. Or maybe the job really was so wretched that you lack the desire to make any change to get offered anything similar.

Save it: save comments in a pending file if there was feedback about something you feel you might want to change. You could have been told about something like personal qualities, actual qualifications or approach that you know you could change or improve, but about which you want to make a more tempered decision. Is their evaluation general or specific to your job or perception? For instance, you could have applied for an internal promotion for a leadership role. You could be told that you missed out because your approach wasn't aggressive or decisive enough. But you could hold strong views and values about the leadership role that don't involve being aggressive or opinionated. Save the thought and consider it later. Maybe you want to try other firms to see if the opinion is shared, in which case you might want to re-evaluate, in case you're coming across as a hopeless ditherer.

Recycle it: these are the evaluations that you can use to help you improve. They're the points made by people whose opinions you value or who clearly know more about the area than you do. They can range from the sublime to the less-than-sublime. You could be told you're too defensive and as a result choose to make changes to your communications and approach. You could be told that you sounded unsure over some of the questions, in which case you will go over those questions and ensure you have a first-class answer next time. Or you could be told that you weren't smart enough, in which case you're going to have to buy or borrow a tie.

Let's imagine you've been on 10 interviews so far and none of them has come up with a sniff of an offer. Now might be a good time to examine your feelings and responses.

Getting your own way

Much of what you do next is connected to what you used to do if you didn't get your own way as a kid. Children look at simple behaviour patterns based on expenditure versus reward, using options such as:

- crying
- sulking
- tantrums
- running away
- getting a hug from mum.

You're an adult, but your response to interview rejection is probably very similar, i.e. you might have adapted your behaviours yet still:

- cry because you're clearly one of life's losers and incapable of getting a job
- sit alone in your room playing Leonard Cohen or Morrisey
- get angry and rant about the interviewers, issuing all sorts of wild threats involving your kneecap and their genitalia
- say you're never going on another interview again – ever!
- get a hug from your partner, mum, dog or total stranger.

It is vitally important that you cast an objective eye over these behaviour options. They might have worked at the most simplistic level when you were 6 years old. Your shopping mall tantrum *might* have been rewarded with a bar of chocolate, but it's not chocolate you're after now, it's a job. Human adults have one huge advantage over animals, which is that we have the ability to be strategic. You have the ability to sit back and look at what's cheesily called the **bigger picture**.

We can see further and we can understand the limitations of the kind of short-term terror tactics we employed when we were 5 years old. These patterns of behaviour will be self-scuppering. Your sulking, denial, anger or even tears are likely to make your interview skills blunter rather than sharper. You can learn two things from an interview rejection – either:

- I'm complete pants and should stop making the effort, or
- I know how to do better next time.

You decide

Rejection is a miserable thing and going on job interviews means courting rejection. Your ego will be screaming 'No! Not again!' even as your fingers type out your CV or resume. Surely the amount of pain felt when you do get turned down for that job is directly proportionate to the amount of effort you invested trying to get it? Maybe so, but that should never teach you to make less effort in the hope that it will hurt less if you get turned down. There might seem to be a logic in this thought but there isn't, I promise you. Trying less hard will only increase your chances of rejection.

I once went on an interview at a woman's magazine. The editor who interviewed me had a face like a slapped arse and kept wiping her nose on a roll of toilet paper. After 20 minutes she informed me I was too old for the job. I was 29 at the time and I nearly spent my 30th birthday in Holloway because of the sudden desire to hurt her in the most painful way possible. I had a folder of work and a head full of ideas. I'd done research and rehearsed my script. I'd even waxed my legs, for God's sake! I left the building vowing I'd never put that amount of effort into an interview again. In future *they'd* have to do the running and I'd treat the job circuit like speed-dating, picking my way through offers in a ruthless and reckless fashion.

Thankfully – once the red mist cleared – I saw the flaw in this line of thinking. Was I really happy to allow that wretched scumbag of a woman to scupper my entire career? No! I carried on trying my best every time, putting maximum effort into every interview. And where is that woman now? I have no idea but I do know that magazine is no longer in circulation.

Try your best or try your *worst*

Either you keep trying your best, regardless. Or you carry on trying and sulk at the same time. Try your *worst*, if your like, or at least try your second or third best. Like agreeing to run in an Olympic race but then not really running very fast. Why would you do that? Well, many people do, with the idea being: 'if I try less hard, then any rejection won't hurt so much'. Like going on a date with Brad Pitt with body odour and a hairy top lip because it will make you feel better when he doesn't ring to take you out again. 'Ha! I didn't really try on that date, if I had done he'd never have looked twice at Angelina Jolie!'. Keep trying your best – it's the only way that makes sense!

Creating an airbag for rejection

Cars aren't designed to crash and you're not going to attend interviews expecting to be rejected ... however, car manufacturers do work on a 'worst-case scenario' survival design that involves things like roll bars and air bags. The manufacturers know that, statistically, a lot of drivers do prang or crash their cars and so adding safety fittings like these will save lives. Similarly, you will know that most interviews – statistically – result in rejection and so it's wise to plan for this to prevent it becoming more than just collateral damage.

Rejection airbagging is relatively easy. Here are some vital tips:

Cancel and continue. This handy little bite-size mantra comes from the acting profession and sporting world. I once interviewed an actor about stage fright and she told me this is the way actors ensure one forgotten line or moment of nerves doesn't affect the rest of the performance. An ice-dancer told me the same thing: 'when you take a tumble in competition you have to leap up and carry on as though nothing has happened, otherwise you could trail that fall with you through the rest of the routine.' So they use a handy brain-trick. **Cancel** ... **Continue** ... **Move on**. It's a reminder not to dwell on an error or moment of failure. There was even a song dedicated to the sentiment: 'Pick yourself up, dust yourself off and start all over again ...'

Dealing with a losing run or even one interview rejection isn't exactly a jolly experience. But your 'cancel and continue' mantra can prevent a hiccup on your career trail turning into a full-blown, 10-act Greek tragedy.

Move on. Change what you can (if you always do what you've always done you'll always get what you've always got!) but then move forward. Never dwell on things you can't change or imagined reasons for rejection. Never get angry. Never marinate in misery. Soldiers never spend time mourning colleagues when the battle's still going on. If they do they get killed. Guess what? You're not going to be an interview casualty because you're going to keep moving. Duck, dive, walk or run but keep moving forward and don't look back once you've evaluated any need for change.

Create a get-out clause that won't scupper your actual performance. Thinking thoughts like: 'I know I won't get this, there are too many good people applying' will vacuum up your confidence and take the form of a sick note, meaning you'll be preparing to fail. Instead, post a thought in your mind along the lines of: 'I could be too well qualified' or 'I know it's sometimes difficult for attractive people to get the best jobs.' By implying to yourself that you could lose out through being too talented or too gorgeous you can keep that ego in full fighting fettle.

Hide a tree in a forest. If you only go to one interview or apply for one post all your hopes will be pinned on that one job. Rejection will then hurt 20 times harder than it would if you'd applied to loads. This is one of the only occasions in life where the collective pain of lots of hurt is less than the sum of one overall blow. Perhaps it's more of an inoculation programme.

When you walk out of your interview tell yourself: 'I could do better than this job/company.' By pointing your thinking onwards and upwards you'll already have left that job offer or lack of it lying in your trail. There are always better companies than the one you've just been interviewed by.

Never use the 'f' word when you talk or think about your interview. Of course I'm not referring to the 'f**k' word but a far worse term which is 'f**l' – **fail**! There's a huge problems with 'fail' thinking – it's technically incorrect. If you didn't get that job you haven't failed. The only real way to fail is when you either don't try or give up. By attending any interview you're making yourself part of a successful process. The word 'fail' is like elastic. Before long it will have stretched and you'll find yourself using the word 'failure' to refer to yourself. If I use the term 'unhelpful' to apply to these types of thoughts, I'm being polite.

Contagious rejection

Did you know rejection is contagious? One turn-down can lead to a whole flurry of others. To see how this theory works, watch a street distributor in action. He or she might be happily giving away free newspapers to passing shoppers or commuters but the minute one passer-by rejects a paper the next few people will also say no. This is the contagious rejection theory in practice. Why did it happen? It's not possible that those first few people did want the paper but – coincidentally – the next crowd didn't. What happened was that one rejection had a profound effect on the entire transaction. The next person saw the rejection and followed like a sheep, meaning the ones after than and the ones after that saw this as the norm behaviour.

The biggest effect is on the distributor. If he or she makes no change to his or her body language and approach, there will be more and more rejection. By pausing, taking stock and then approaching the next passer-by with renewed energy, positivity and enthusiasm, looking as if they're expected to take the paper rather than turn it down, the distributor should find it easy to break the chain of 'contagious rejection'.

The same will apply to your interviews. Take a previous turn-down into your next interview, either via a more cautious attitude or negative-looking body language signals – and you could scupper any chances of success going forward.

How to be a more motivated person

Motivated people tend to have six key things in common and you can copy them easily.

1. **They focus on their goals.** Keep reminding yourself where you're going and what you want to get. The interview process is a means to an end, not the end itself.
2. **They remind themselves of their goals on a regular basis.** It's easier to work through any process-pain if you have a strong image in your mind of the end result. Remember when you learned how to drive? You got through any anxiety or effort by seeing yourself driving alone in a new car. You might have imagined all the dates it would get you or the freedom to travel. Your reality is the job or career you're after and what that job will enable you to achieve or enjoy (such as a new house or holidays). Visual prompts are very powerful. Many successful people told me they have a photograph of the thing they want most pinned above their desk or stuck on their fridge door to remind them why they're doing what they do.
3. **They accept the fact that it won't be easy.** For many motivated people the pain is what it's all about. No pain – no gain, all that sort of thing.

4. **They don't accept 'no' or 'can't'.** Most of us lesser mortals will lie down and play dead at the first knock-back or even the first *sniff* of a possible knock-back.
5. **They coach themselves.** Self-motivation is key. Being motivated means not wandering around wailing and waiting to be picked up by someone else, like a kid who's grazed his knee.
6. **They write lists.** Messages of commitment to themselves. To-do lists, lists of goals and lists of achievements and self-praise. Some of them even write notes from their positive selves to their not-so-positive selves in advance. This means sitting down before the fight to write motivational messages to yourself while you're strong to keep you going if or when you need it. This self-picking-self-up can work wonders as a restorative, miles better than listening to adages and waffle from well-meaning partners or friends who might appear like smug know-it-alls on the day.

Re-motivate when life sucks!

Your ego would need to have balls of steel to face interview turn-downs with a smile and a cheery wave. It hurts, of course it hurts. You've offered yourself up, all suited, booted and smiley and somebody has said 'no thanks'. Or maybe several firms have said 'no thanks'. Perhaps loads of them. If being made redundant feels like being jilted, then interview turn-downs feel like being stood up on a first date or – maybe worse – having a marriage proposal turned down after a long courtship (in the case of applying for internal promotion).

To be blunt, you're presented with two choices:

1. Keep trying …
2. Give up.

You're going with the first option, so give it your best shot. Every interview is an opportunity to change your life. Never miss an opportunity because the last one that came along didn't work out. Never try your worst!

IN A NUTSHELL

- When you can't control the stimulus, work to take control over your response.
- Take an objective view of what went wrong: use your checklist to assess what you did, what you said and how your behaved.
- Work to improve, rather than sulking or self-scuppering.
- Bin it, Save it or Recycle it: the three methods of dealing with rejection.
- Try your best: don't try your *worst*.
- Train your brain to cancel and continue.
- Follow the six golden rules of motivated people.

6 IMPRESSION MANAGEMENT

How to create powerful communications and lasting impact and image

This chapter explains how the way you are perceived can be crucial to your interview success and shows how to make sure your impression works for you rather than against you by:

- understanding the processes of the **first impression** and how you are assessed in the first few seconds of meeting
- explaining the psychology of interview communications and the impact of the way you put your messages across
- working on your interview etiquette skills
- giving tips on your body language, tone of voice and use of words to make sure your communications have impact and style
- helping to make sure all your communications are clear and concise.

Instant impact

Much of the information you relay about yourself during an interview will be transmitted during the first four seconds. This is known as the **first impression** and it's largely a subconscious process. We see someone, and straight away we begin to decide whether we approve of them or not.

Your first impression is created by these seven key factors.

- your eye contact and gaze
- your facial expressions
- your posture
- your gestures
- touch
- spatial behaviour
- grooming and dress.

OK, so this is an unfair process. Most of it appears based on superficiality, bias and stereotype. However, it is part of your survival processes. Animals need to read other animals and their intentions very quickly and they don't do it by exchanging verbal pleasantries. The first impression is part of your evolutionary processing and therefore impossible to suppress. You'll be judged on your visual signals whether you like it or not, so it makes sense for you to ensure your face fits.

Silent speech

Your body language will talk for you even when your mouth is shut!

Do you know how important your body language signals are during a recruitment interview? In any face-to-face communication your **non-verbal signals** account for around 55% of the perceived impact of your messages. Your **tone of voice** accounts for about 38%, which leaves a measly 7% for your actual words. Put simply then, it isn't what you say but the *way* that you say it that counts!

Why is body language so high? Two reasons.

We remember what we see far longer than the words we hear. Ever watch all those politicians campaigning for an election? I doubt you remember much that they said but I promise you'd be swayed by the way their hands moved, arms flailed or the smile they were wearing while they said it. Many years ago a politician called Michael Foot learned this lesson the hard way. Although he was acknowledged as a very able politician his habit of wearing casual, workman's jackets to formal occasions and having a head of long, wild white hair made his tenure at the top very brief.

We tend to believe gestures and other visual signals more than we do the spoken word. People lie at interviews and it's far easier to lie with your words than it is with your gestures. Body language is one hell of a big giveaway!

It's easy to use that feeling of discomfort and awkwardness you'll feel when you first become 'bodytalk aware' but you really do ignore your own body language signals at your peril. By 'being yourself' and failing to spend some time honing and improving all those gestures and facial expressions you'll be doing the equivalent to allowing words to spill out of your mouth without using tact, care or strategy planning.

Your body language should be worked on for two core reasons.

1. **Etiquette:** an interview is a business ritual and every ritual comes complete with its own etiquette rules.
2. **Self-marketing:** making a good impression means using your body language to endorse your words. Your body language will give you impact at interview stage and it will help create your charisma (or lack of it!).

Etiquette rules: OK?

As far as your charm charisma is concerned, you'll need to ensure you have all these five key interview stages taken care of:

1. arrival in reception
2. meetings and greetings
3. eating and drinking
4. networking
5. departures.

Arriving

When you arrive for your interview make sure you do the following.

- When you phone ahead of your visit, ask if there are parking facilities or whether you're likely to be delayed by security scanning etc. Explain this is to enable you to estimate ideal arrival time.

- Arrive 10 minutes before the interview.
- Give your name to the receptionist, plus the name of the person you have your appointment with and the time of your appointment.
- Switch off your mobile phone while you're waiting.
- If you're late always phone ahead and explain how late you're likely to be and the reason for your delay. Apologise! Apologise again during the greeting process.
- Sit quietly in reception. Read a newspaper if they're available but fold it nicely again once you've finished.
- Never eat food or drink in reception unless there is a coffee outlet. Even then it's better to wait.
- If other people arrive in reception it's polite to nod and smile at them as they take a seat.
- If you feel the delay in reception has been suspiciously long don't display impatience, i.e. puffing, fidgeting and looking at your watch. A few minutes after the planned interview time feel free to walk up to reception and politely ask whether they said how long it might be before you're called.
- You can ask the receptionist if you need to use the toilet.
- The person who comes to meet you in reception could be an interviewer but he or she could also be a personal assistant. Try not to make assumptions and listen when they introduce themselves.
- Always stand up to receive a handshake.
- The host should instigate the handshake. Wait for them to offer their hand and if they don't – don't shake at all.
- Shake with your right hand.
- They should say something like: 'Carol Smith? I'm Pete Brown, Sara Holt's PA.' If they say your name first then your response should be 'Pleased to meet you.' If they don't, say: 'Carol Smith, pleased to meet you'.
- They might lead as you walk towards the office but expect them to motion for you to enter the lift first. Remember there is no difference between men and women when it comes to business etiquette. In matters of who opens door for who the best answer is: whoever gets there first!
- If they offer to carry a bag for you, it's polite to say 'No, thank you, I'm fine'.
- Repeat the handshaking ritual with all the interviewers when you are shown into the interview room. Leave no one out.
- Wait to be offered a seat. If no one offers, ask before you sit down.
- You can adjust the angle of the chair but don't move it too much – it looks rude, especially if you pull it right up to the desk.

- Don't touch, lean on or place bags on their desk. If it's a board table you can place an elbow or hands on it.
- If you're offered tea or coffee don't ask for anything else. 'I don't drink tea or coffee, can I have a water?' sounds rude. It's not a café.
- If you're giving out business cards only offer them at the end of the interview but not at all if they've got your CV.
- Never take your suit jacket off, especially if they leave theirs on.
- Never chew gum.
- Never glance at your watch or a text.
- Expect to shake hands again when the interview is over. Thank each person as you do so.
- Thank the receptionist on the way out.

Eating and drinking

Modern businesses often have their own large cafés or restaurants and like to host candidates over food and drink. One glance into the reception areas of top City companies will often reveal a coffee outlet to rival anything in the high street, meaning your social skills will be on display. Is it paranoid to think that you might lose a job because you buttered your bread roll in the wrong way or got a latte froth moustache? I don't think so. I have personal experience of companies that like to vet candidates with the view that they will be required to wine and dine clients if they do get the job. Some later stages of interview can often take place over dinner at a restaurant or hotel. Knowing your way around the etiquette rules can therefore be vital.

If you're nervous it might be wise to refuse offers of drinks during your interview. Shaky hands can lead to spillage!

You might be offered a canteen lunch with other interviewees. Allow other people to queue in front of you rather than rushing to the top of the queue and don't fill your plate as if you're there for the free food. Try not to take more than your host. Sitting with a plate of hot chilli while they're picking at a tuna sandwich looks bad.

DO: pick food that is easy to eat.

DO: wait for the host to start eating. This is even more crucial for a formal meal.

DON'T: 'fill up' with the bread rolls at a formal dinner. Break small pieces off your roll as you eat your food but don't polish it off before you eat and then take another.

DO: lay your napkin on your lap. In a posh restaurant a waiter might do this for you.

DO: eat something at each course but only if your host instigates it. For instance if he or she skips the starter you should do the same.

DO: avoid drinking alcohol and *never* order alcohol if your host sticks to water.

DO: start with the outside cutlery and work inwards.

DON'T: talk or eat with your mouth open and never criticise the food or pull faces. Even if they have tripe, offal or monkey brains on the menu, carry on smiling. You don't have to order it or eat it.

Shaking hands

The handshake has it roots in simian behaviours. A threatened ape will often offer its paw out to a stronger ape as a signal of appeasement and submission. In human behaviours, this has become the mutual offering of the hand and a gesture of mutual submission. So what you're really saying in animal terms is: 'let's agree to not fight'. What this means is that your handshake should be open and confident. A half-offered hand where the palms don't actually touch will feel like a guarded signal that can even appear threatening, as if you're holding something back!

- Never squeeze or crush the interviewer's hand.
- Be prepared to shake with everyone you meet at the firm.
- Never offer a 'dead fish', i.e. a soggy, floppy handshake.
- Never wipe your hand on your trousers before you offer it (i.e. in full sight).
- Shake at just below waist height.
- The hands should go up and down about three times.
- Let the interviewer both instigate and end the shake.
- Always mirror the shake you're offered – if theirs is firmer, firm yours up a little, if it's speedy, reply in kind.
- Never take their hand in both of yours (known as the **hand sandwich**).
- Never touch them on the arm as you shake.
- Always get up to shake hands.
- Always make the most of this ritual. It's an important one that should be savoured rather than hurried.

HOW TO SHAKE HANDS

Your handshake will reveal a lot about your personality and attitude. In many ways it's like your own personal chip and pin. It's the ritual that comes at the two key moments of any interview – the start and the finish – so it's vital you ensure your handshake both creates and leaves the right impression. How many times have you been introduced to someone whose handshake has made them appear either weak and submissive or over-dominant?

- Arrive with your coat and/or bags carried in your left hand so your right is free to shake.
- Make eye contact as you shake.
- Smile!
- Lean forward very slightly into the shake.
- Offer a dry, firm hand.

- Not all cultures shake hands. If your interviewer doesn't shake, it could be a nationality thing.
- If you know the company you're visiting is foreign, look out for different forms of greeting, like the bow.

It is rare to be kissed on the cheek at a first interview but if your interview is for an internal promotion you might know your interviewer well already. Cheek-kissing has a way of getting clumsy, especially if you feel nervous or under pressure. If you see one coming, touch lightly on both shoulders and kiss right cheeks first, then left. Never make a loud 'Mwa!' sound as it could appear sarcastic!

Networking techniques

It's quite common for a large company to invite applicants to some form of social or networking event. This is seen as a useful way to mingle in a more informal manner and often to have talks from different managers about the company or their department. These events might appear to involve you in an 'audience' role, listening to talks and standing about drinking cups of tea, but most companies who hold them will also see them as a form of mass interview too, picking out applicants who seem to have the appropriate skills of mingling, communicating and self-promotion.

If you are asked to attend a session like this, or even if you're taken for a chat over tea during your more formal interview, do see this as very much part of the interview itself and take a proactive and active role, rather than just standing around waiting to be spoken to. There's no need to rush about sucking up to anyone with a company name-badge but do employ good mingling techniques to promote your cause and show how well your face would fit in the company line-up.

Learn how to 'do the room'. Your job is to work your way around all the guests, chatting for most of them for a small space of time.

Pause before you walk in. Pull yourself to full height, pull your shoulders back and down, shake your hands a little to release tension, relax your facial expression and think of something that will make you smile in a natural way (imagine you're walking into a room full of your friends).

Once you enter the room, pause for no longer than three seconds to look around and take stock. A host might approach you, in which case return the handshake and introduce yourself, even if you're wearing a name badge. Ask the host who you should meet first and with luck they'll give you names and point people out, or even introduce you. If there's no host on tap, grab a tea or water and go across to the nearest person or group.

If you're breaking into a group try to choose a group of three or more but no larger than six (a pair is often harder to break up and large numbers will mean you get lost).

Approach the group with a purposeful walk and a confident facial expression, never look as if you're lurking about. Look for the largest gap and stand in it.

You might find the group doesn't open to accept you (it happens!) If so, wait for no longer than one or two seconds before waving to a pretend friend across the other side of the room and walking off to try somewhere else.

If you get in a gap, glance quickly at the people on either side, nodding at them slightly before joining in the conversation.

Always tune into the group's existing dynamics before plunging in. They won't welcome you changing their mood.

If someone is speaking, wait until they've finished. While you wait, use your mirroring techniques to ingratiate yourself and earn acceptance. Match the group's overall mood and body language. If it's relaxed and light hearted laugh along with them, even if you didn't hear the start of the joke. If it's more formal and serious follow suit.

Once the current speaker has finished, tie your own words in with theirs as in 'Was that Surrey University you were talking about? That's really interesting, I found they had a lot to offer to anyone with scientific skills too', then ... 'By the way, my name's Jack Smith.'

Be reasonably aggressive in your mingling techniques. If you find you're chatting to someone with little relevance to your objective (to get a job offer!) don't stay with them for ages just because you find them easy to talk to. Either be blunt – 'it was great meeting you now I ought to get off and carry on mingling' – or nicer – 'now, who do you think we ought to be introducing ourselves to? Have you spoken to anyone else from the company?'

Make sure any potential interviewers get to hear your name clearly during introductions. There's no need to shout but do enunciate well!

Ask questions about the company as it will make you sound keen, but avoid questions about money, pay rises or bonuses as they'll think you're only interested in the dosh, not the job itself.

If they're telling you about the company or its history you must avoid boredom displays, even the subtlest ones. No yawning, looking at your watch, glancing around the room, slyly checking your phone, face-touching, fiddling, glazed eyes or sighing. Never use the words: 'oh that sounds really interesting ...', as it's impossible to say this without sounding terminally bored (which you could well be). Instead, use the reflecting technique:

- **Interviewer:** The company was founded in Swansea in 1998 by Barry Harmsworth and Bill Neath
- **You:** Nineteen ninety-eight?

This simple technique shows that you're listening and are keen to hear more.

Always use displays of active listening.

HOW TO SHOW ACTIVE LISTENING SIGNALS

- Use 100% eye contact.
- Lean forward slightly.
- Tilt your head slightly to one side at some stage while you're listening.
- Nod.
- Pace your nod to their delivery, i.e. fast nods for a funny story, slower for a more businesslike delivery and very slow for bad news.
- Never nod too quickly: it signals impatience and a desire to interrupt.
- Mirror the speaker's body language to create rapport: but be subtle!
- Let your facial expression reflect their story.
- Be careful about mirroring their facial expression without listening to their content. People often laugh or smile when they're delivering bad news.
- Never face-touch, it can signal boredom.
- Apart from a bent-finger-under-chin gesture, which can signal genuine interest.
- Never rest your chin in the palm of your hand: it will look as if you're about to nod off!
- Never place one finger up the side of your face: it will make you look judgemental or distrustful.
- Maintain a steady blink-rate. Accelerated blinking can make you appear bored.
- Face the speaker front and full-on.

Leaving

Leaving the room at the end of an interview can take almost as much planning as making your entrance. In many ways this can be your 'Mr Bean' moment, the part of the meeting when your control and charisma suddenly slip away and you're left bumbling, stumbling and uttering ghastly clichés as you make your way to the door.

Exit handshakes are more difficult than the arrival ones as there's also the door to manoeuvre. And although you might have sashayed into the room with all the cool charm you could muster, picking your things up again and quitting with that last *bon mot* might be a serious challenge to your otherwise nifty choreography.

Let them announce when it's time for you to leave. Try to spot visual cues, like leaning back from the desk or placing the hands palm-down onto the desk and smiling.

Don't suddenly try to talk for England. Once your time is up it's better to go. In time terms, it's only too easy to talk yourself out of a job by over-yapping in a bid to stay for longer.

Think before you rise from your chair. Are there bags or papers on your lap? Or tucked down by your side? Did you accidentally place a coffee cup on the floor by your feet? Where is your coat? Never push your chair back without first checking the area.

If they start to shake hands the same rule applies as for arrivals: the host instigates the shake. If their hand goes out too soon, don't do the 'crouch-and-shake' where you're only partly out of your chair, clutching bags to your lap and try to move across to grab their hand as well (more common than you might think!). Stand upright, pause a second, then step across to take their hand.

If they remain behind the desk, you should walk to the doors then pause before quitting, turn around and smile and thank them before you leave.

If they walk you to the door, they might open the door but you should walk through first. If they walk you back to reception, turn to shake hands as you get to the main exit.

Many larger companies have quite a complex security system involving electronic passes. If you were given a plastic visitor's card or a badge on the way into the building make sure you hand it back to reception on the way out and thank them as you do so.

How to impress the interviewers

This section of the book is about using your body language signals to increase your chances of getting a job offer. There is no 'one-size-fits-all' when it comes to impressive image; each company and each interviewer will have their own idea of what an 'ideal' candidate looks like. However, there are some powerful techniques that you can learn and use that will help you to maximise your personal impact.

Put in a lot of work and effort to make it look as if you're not trying too hard. It is tragic if your body language looks too rehearsed and unnatural, but that doesn't mean you should ignore it and just do your own thing. You're going to take part in an unnatural situation. If you sit as you normally do, dress as you normally dress and communicate in your normal way, the odds are they either won't understand what you're telling them or they'll think you look awkward and ungainly. Everyone in the public eye will spend some time (and perhaps a lot of time) getting their image right. Your interview is a performance of sorts and any performer will succeed and fail on two things:

1. the amount of talent they have
2. the amount of practice and rehearsal they put in.

The first step in modifying your body language is the same first step you should use when deciding what words to choose when you speak to someone.

Know your goals

Imagine you will be walking into that interview room wearing a large T-shirt with your ideal words to describe you written across the front in big letters. What words would you choose to wear on that T-shirt? How would you like to be perceived? What image would you want to present to the interviewer?

When you plan your image strategy, pick positive qualities rather than focusing on the negatives: it's a very good brain-training technique. The brain never hears the words 'don't', it only accepts the command, so if your T-shirt message is 'Don't look nervous' it's only the last word in that message that will be absorbed, meaning you will be more likely to look nervous than you were before you made up your slogan.

So – how about:

confident knowledgeable
keen experienced?

The next step is to decide exactly how each of those T-shirt qualities would look. As always in this book, the key message is: **show, don't tell!**

How can you show you're capable of being a confident member of their staff rather than telling them? Here's a run-down of the most common ideal image objectives and competencies at an interview, plus a list of qualities you will want to avoid. The idea of listing the body language symptoms is to enable you to mix and match as required. Not all interviews will demand the same set of competencies, so it's important you tailor your messages to suit company and job requirements.

How to look confident

- Present a natural-looking, relaxed smile (see page 000).
- Carry yourself at full height with shoulders pulled back and down.
- Use eye contact but don't overdo it! Soften your eye expression to avoid turning your gaze into a glassy stare!
- Keep your head up with your chin at a 45-degree angle to your neck.
- Move quickly and with energy but don't rush.
- Avoid body-barrier gestures like folded arms or clutching at a shoulder bag.
- But do cross your legs when you sit down if you want to.
- Use open, emphatic gestures as you talk.
- Avoid fiddling with jewellery, hair or pens.
- Avoid leg-judder! Or foot-tapping.
- Try to sit reasonably still, although don't look like a dummy!
- Keep your hand gestures below shoulder height and above waist height.

How to display power and status

- Use emphatic gestures as you talk.
- Be spatial. Place your arms onto the arms on your chair, or place your hand onto the board table.
- Use eye contact.
- Use steepling hand gestures (fingers joined at the tips).
- Gesticulate more than the interviewer.
- Use head-baton gestures, i.e. nod your head with authority to emphasise your key words.
- Lean back in your seat but lean forward to present your key points.

How to persuade and influence

- Lock into the interviewer's core communications style and copy it subtly.

- Use mirroring, i.e. subtly copying his or her body language to fast-track rapport and empathy.
- Use active listening signals like nodding and eye contact to display respect and interest.
- Pace your listening nods to the rhythm of their speech.
- Flex your own communication style to be compatible with theirs. Are they concise? High in impact? Using emphatic gestures and lots of eye contact? Do they skip the small talk and get straight to the point? If so, they are a **driver**.
- Respond with a clear, emphatic speaking style and confident, open gestures. Never waffle! A 'driving' communicator relishes status, so avoid challenging him or her or appearing more confident or high status than they do.
- Are they smiling, friendly and concerned with your well-being, offering tea, biscuits and listening carefully as you talk? If so, they could be an **empathist**. This means their communication style focuses on the personality and relationship side of the interview and they find small talk and your background very important. Smile back, nod to show you're listening, don't interrupt or sound or look arrogant and never complain about previous employers or workmates. These people value trust and honesty very highly indeed, so avoid looking as if you're exaggerating or being dishonest in any way.
- Do they ooze personality, enthusiasm and energy? Do they adopt a jokey style of communication, using large, open gestures? If so, they could be a **performer**. These people love energy and enthusiasm in other people and like to be the centre of attention. Laugh at their jokes but don't try to top them. Talk about your talents, as they're not very motivated by facts and figures on paper so may have skip-read your CV.
- Or are they quieter and softly-spoken but very concerned with detail, dates and logic? If so he or she could be an **analyst**. These people are low on performance but high on facts and figures. Enthusiastic body language is still important but much less so than if you're dealing with a **performer**. These people will only really be impressed by evidence and proof, not thoughts, feelings and opinions.

How to look keen

- Walk into the office with energy, keeping a focused eye expression.
- Don't bounce! Bouncing or skipping will make you look like an idiot.
- Sit slightly forward in your chair, elbows on the arms of the chair.
- Nod as they speak, pacing your nods to their speech.
- Widen your eyes now and again and raise your brows.
- Use eye contact with each person who addresses you during the interview.
- As you talk use gestures that involve subtle palm displays.
- Never fold your arms.
- Always take a good-quality pen and some professional-looking paper or a notebook with you. If it feels appropriate, take notes if you need to. This implies you intend to act on information they're giving you or at least that you're making a genuine effort to remember it.
- Have a business card. But be careful. Never look too flash with your cards. The good news is they're quite cheap to get printed or you could print your own on your PC. Keep them very simple, and never give it out until the end of the interview, not at the beginning.

How to look knowledgeable

- Lean forward as you're being asked a question. This will imply you have the ability to answer any question they might throw at you.
- Never answer too quickly. This will make it sound as if the questions are too easy. Take a small pause before you answer and allow your eyes to flick down and to your left. This will imply the question is stretching and intelligent and that you are thinking before you answer.
- Never allow your eyes to flick upward. This can imply you're in need of some help and on the brink of panic!
- Avoid self-comfort rituals like fiddling, scratching or self-hugging (tightly folded arms).
- Do display both your hands as you're being interviewed. Never sit with them on your lap if that means they aren't visible behind a desk or board table. If you're sitting at a desk place your arms onto the arms of your chair and if you're sitting around a board table place your hands on the table.
- Use emphatic gestures as you speak. Never throw your arms around or use jerky, irrelevant gestures.
- Use **precision gestures** as you make your points. One of the best is an upward-pointing finger-pinch. Simply touch your fingertips against your thumb-tip and lift your hand up and down a few times as you speak.

- Breathe out slowly to relax your body and to drop your vocal tone slightly. People equate intelligence with a slightly deeper vocal tone.
- Never try to bluff if you've been asked a tricky question and don't know the answer. Your body language will be a give-away, and looking as if you're lying won't make the interviewers believe you're knowledgeable. Honesty is the best policy. Keep cool, use eye contact and lean forward slightly towards your questioner. Tell them you don't know the answer, or ask them to re-phrase it if you find their words confusing.
- Smile politely each time you're asked a question. It will look as if you enjoy the experience.
- Avoid defensive-looking gestures like reeling back from a question, folding your arms, face-touching, head-scratching, sucking your lips inward, chewing your lip, fast-blinking and darting eyes.

How to look approachable

- Shyness can look attractive but not if it makes you look disconnected or distracted. Don't allow your head to dip or your hair to fall over your face. And avoid eye 'cut-offs' i.e. looking anywhere but at the interviewer's face.
- Employ good, friendly eye contact from the moment you walk into the room. Remember to keep the eye expression softened, giving the effect of smiling with your eyes.
- Lean forward slightly to greet people.
- Move quickly across the room to shake the interviewers by the hand. Although they should instigate the shake you should put energy and effort into performing it, rather than just standing there, waiting.
- Repeat people's names after being introduced to let them know you're making an effort to remember them.
- Use a congruent (genuine)-looking smile. Make sure it starts with the eyes, then works down the face. Remember a smile spreads quite slowly. If you perform a 'lightning' smile – one that appears, then disappears too quickly – it will look insincere.
- Greet interviewers facing full-frontal.
- When you meet and greet, don't do anything to appear distracted. Make meeting the interviewers look like the only thing on your mind.
- Don't attempt to rush the greeting rituals.
- Use active listening signals (see page 88).

Looks to avoid

Looking arrogant

- Splaying, i.e. standing or sitting with your legs thrown too far apart.
- Keeping your head held too high so that your chin is up and you appear to be looking down your nose.
- Closing your eyes as you talk (apart from blinking, obviously).
- Smug smiling, i.e. a lop-sided smile with your lips closed.
- Steepling, i.e. sitting with your fingertips touching and pointed upward.
- Raising one eyebrow.
- Raising both brows in an 'eye-shrug' when you're asked a question, implying it's an odd question to ask.
- Shrugging with your shoulders.
- Rolling your eyes.
- Sighing before you answer a question.
- Sitting slumped down in your chair.
- Sitting down before being asked to.
- Being the first one to offer your hand to be shaken.
- Patting as you shake.

Looking aggressive

- Folding your arms high up on your chest.
- Pointing as you talk.
- Making chopping gestures with your hands.
- Holding your hand up with the palm facing the interviewer in a 'halt' gesture.
- Sprawling in your seat.
- Crossing one leg across the other with one calf resting on the other thigh.
- Tapping your feet or fingers.
- Cracking your knuckles.
- Staring.
- Narrowing your eyes.
- Jutting your jaw.
- Using a stretched-looking smile with a lot of tooth display.
- Sticking or puffing your chest out.
- Wobbling your head from side to side.
- Chewing your nails or lips (self-attacks like this can signal suppressed aggression).
- Sniffing.
- Looking over the top of your spectacles.

- Sucking your teeth.
- Chewing gum.
- Puffing.
- Sitting with your hands behind your head.
- Putting your hand or hands on your hips.

Congruence

The best body language signals are ones that endorse or emphasise your words, making you appear genuine, open and honest. When you speak normally your gestures will appear just before your words, as it's easier for humans to communicate via body movement than via speech, so gestures that occur just after your words risk making you look insincere.

Most body language analysis is subliminal. Although some interviewers do like to pride themselves on being body language 'experts' (notice my use of inverted commas there) the majority will put the impressions they form about you and your personality down to instinct or gut reaction. So when I say that speaking before you gesture could make you look insincere I don't mean your interviewer will pull out his or her 'I-Spy Book of Body Language' to analyse your signals in individual detail but they will make an 'eye evaluation', possibly without knowing they're doing it.

If your words and your non-verbal signal marry up, it's possible you will look as if you mean what you say. So if you're telling the interviewer you really do want the job and you nod slightly, use eye contact and use open gestures they will probably believe you. But if you're shaking your head, fiddling or looking bored as you say it you'll be doing what's called an **incongruent display,** which will send out mixed signals. And when your gestures contradict your words like this it's usually the gestures that are assessed as being harder to adjust and therefore more reliable. Plus people do tend to remember what they see longer than what they hear.

Changing your body language

Does the thought of changing your body language make you feel self-conscious and awkward? If you're thinking that postural or gestural change is the last thing you'll want to be thinking about when you're under pressure at an interview, you're in good company. Self-awareness creates discomfort. When animals feel uncomfortable, the most natural option is to return to their zone of comfort. Logically this might sound like giving up and forgetting about your own physical signals again, or returning to a state of unconscious error, as the psychologists would call it.

However, there is another option: work on your body language techniques before the interview. Improve, rehearse, grow. Stick with that change. After a very short period of time it will be within the scope of your new zone of comfort. You'll be using your new body language without conscious thought or self-awareness. You could learn an entire dance routine in one weekend. How easy are a few body language tweaks going to be?

Tweaking or major re-sculpting?

Most people I train are easily able to improve their impact and image with a few easy tweaks. You don't need to be aware of every movement as you talk, just a couple of the major ones.

Think of the interviewer's goals for a moment. What does he or she want to see during an interview? There's a strong set of animal values rumbling around, especially if the interview is your first meeting with the interviewer and his or her company. As sophisticated as we like to be in our working lives, much of the visual messaging is to do with the old issues of fight–flight and power and status. Paring it back to basics, most interviewers – apart from your physical or intellectual skills or competencies – will be looking to see if you're:

- **normal:** safe to accept into their pack, colony or tribe
- **keen to assimilate:** showing a desire to ingratiate with their colony
- **acceptable:** showing enough traits to ensure they will be accepted by the existing colony without fight
- **safe:** unthreatening to the existing colony.

These are just the basics. Different jobs come with variable criteria. You could also find they want:

- **external ingratiation skills:** the ability to get on with customers
- **fight skills:** the confidence and strength to create and put through change in the existing colony
- **leadership skills:** the ability to enforce existing standards within the existing colony.

To excel at these basics via your body language signals, all you need is a core understanding of animal behaviours.

Animals have no speech, so they need to show other animals they're encountering for the first time what their intentions are pretty damn quick, with little margin for error. When you attend an interview, your first concerns should be showing to one another that you come in peace. This is where your ingratiation and acceptance begins.

In the simian world this means appropriate signals of rapport – which is why you shake hands. Where a submissive monkey will offer its paw, you'll offer your hand to be shaken. They'll offer theirs first to show higher status.

When you shake, you smile. When an ape wants to make friends it will often pull its lips back slightly from its teeth. If it wants to fight or kill it will pull those lips back fully, in a snarl, and this is why it's important your smile doesn't look false and over-performed!

As the interview progresses, it's important you don't step on the interviewer's toes in status terms. For that moment at least they have alpha status, so using more space, sitting or standing higher and dressing to look smarter or wealthier could be a mistake. Interviewers might not admit it but they rarely enjoy a challenge to their seniority during an interview, which is why your etiquette is so important.

Misdirected mail

It would be highly unusual for you to deliberately create a negative impression during a recruitment interview. However, it is entirely possible to shoot yourself in the foot, in image terms, entirely by accident. How? Well, some sides of your personality might be capable of creating a visual misunderstanding. Take shyness, for instance. There's nothing wrong with being shy. I suffer myself. The problem is that shyness has what doctors call **presenting symptoms** that might lead to the wrong diagnosis. For instance, all that lack of eye contact, fiddling or shuffling might suggest disinterest or even rudeness. Your inability to smile might be read as lack of desire to be sociable or indifference to the occasion. Blushing and sweating can be seen as guilt rather than embarrassment and that uncontrollable giggle might imply severe brain-rot rather than mild intimidation.

So when you work on your body language you won't just be trying to make a good impression by adding signals to your repertoire – confidence, charm, charisma – you'll also be busy erasing any negative ones – boredom, being out of your depth – as well as modifying any that aren't prompted by negative thoughts but that might give a misleading impression – nerves and shyness.

Work that body

It takes less than 30 days to learn a new habit and for your body to consign new movements into **muscle memory**, making it able to perform movements with conscious thought. So any time you have before your next interview shouldn't just be spent rehearsing answers to questions and polishing up your CV.

ACTIVITY 3

LOOK IN THE MIRROR

Get a full-length mirror and place a chair in front of it.

Dress in your interview outfit (if possible) if not, anything along similar lines, like a jacket and shirt. If you're wearing a skirt to your interview please dress accordingly. Body language in trousers is vastly different to body language movements in a skirt.

Stand as far back from the mirror as possible. Ideally it would be great if you could have the mirror facing a door so that you can rehearse your entrance; if not, mime your door.

Pause and take a moment. Pull up to full height, roll your shoulders back and down and breathe out slowly.

As you breathe out, relax your facial expression, starting with the eyes. Imagine you're about to approach your best friend. What sort of eye signals would you use? The look you're aiming for is eye contact, including a friendly 'eye-smile'. One your eye expression is relaxed and confident you can allow your smile to spread to your mouth. Do remember this is consciously creating an expression that will normally occur subconsciously, so don't worry if it looks ghastly the first few times you do it! Keep trying until the face looking back at from the mirror looks vaguely humanoid and then keep working until it appears friendly and approachable.

Keep your shoulders pushed down. Tension causes muscle contraction, which will mean your shoulders rise up in the direction of your ears and your arms from shoulder to elbow can begin to hug themselves to the sides of your ribs. Create a small space between your arms and your body by dropping your shoulders and pushing your elbows out very slightly.

Push your pelvis in and under – but very subtly! This will straighten your back but in a natural-looking way.

Take another look in the mirror. Do you look as if you've just joined the army? If you do then you've over-done things. Relax and start again. You shouldn't look as if you're on parade! Is your chin raised too high? Are you pulling your shoulders back rather than pressing them down? Breathe out slowly and have another go.

Use a business bag as a prop, as it's likely you'll be carrying one when you walk into your interview. Avoid using a bag with a shoulder strap, as they tend to slip about, making you clutch at them. The bag you take shouldn't make it necessary for you to perform any body-crossing gestures with your arm. A briefcase is ideal. Carry it in your left hand, leaving the right free for shaking.

As you walk in through the door (or mime walking in through a door) try to make your entrance without turning your back. Step in through the door, then push it closed behind you while you're still facing the mirror. Smile and relax. It's the most difficult manoeuvre you'll be rehearsing, but it's worth the effort as it will make you look far more charismatic.

Walk forward towards the mirror as if you're approaching an interviewer who is waiting to shake your hand. Extend your own arm, use eye contact and keep the relaxed-looking smile in place. Remember you would probably be talking by now, so try introducing yourself out loud. (We'll tackle verbal introductions and small talk in Chapter 8.)

Now imagine you've been offered a seat. Sit down on the chair you've placed in front of the mirror. Place your bag on the floor beside you as you step back, touching the chair with the back of your leg to check where it is. If you're wearing a skirt, smooth it under your bottom and sit down.

Taking a seat should require two movements. Never throw yourself straight into the back of the chair, sit nearer the front first, then bob back into the back of the chair.

Sit with your back against the back of the chair so that you look confident within the space. If you're short and this means your feet dangle, sit further forward!

Place your elbows onto the arms of the chair and allow your hands to lie loosely in your lap. If there are no arms to your interview chair, you should clasp your hands lightly and place them to the side of your lap.

Cross your legs, but not calf-across-thigh as it looks too arrogant and not crossed at the ankles as it looks prissy.

Or you can sit with your legs medium-space apart but only if you're a bloke!

Never tuck your feet underneath your chair, as it looks like a desire to hide.

Never wrap your feet around the chair legs!

Never cross your legs more than once. If you have short legs this notion might confuse you, but girls with Olive Oyl legs like mine can happily wrap them round one another like a maypole.

Never allow your top leg in the leg cross to swing backwards and forwards.

Never cross your arms or pull your hands right in up to your torso.

Now imagine you're talking. Work on your eye contact (even if you're only miming), looking around from one interviewer to the next as you speak.

Talk into your mirror, answering imagined questions. As you speak, start to gesticulate, using open and emphatic gestures that keep within shoulder and waist height. If you find yourself fiddling or waving your hands around wildly, give your hands and arms a little shake and start again.

Rehearse your back-channel communications: nodding, uh-huh, OK, right, etc. to confirm listening.

If you fiddle with jewellery, take it off and start again.

Now rehearse your listening signals. Imagine your invisible interviewer is talking to you. Use eye contact, nod, head-tilt etc. Then rehearse your 'thinking' pause before you answer their question, looking down and to your left for a moment before coming back with eye contact again.

Once you're on a roll, it's a good idea to rehearse some tricky moments too. Imagine you've been asked a 'killer question'. Lean forward slightly, keep the eye contact but don't turn it into staring. Avoid laughing or looking smug but also don't look defensive or uncomfortable. Pause to think again and then come back with your answer.

Now imagine you've been asked an inappropriate question, say about having children or being married. Rehearse your response and see how it looks. Remember it's their mistake, not yours, so work to eliminate any embarrassment signals like giggling, dropping your chin or over-gesticulating. Keep a steady and confident look. Avoid looking too confrontational or aggressive. Try a polite smile and steady eye contact, plus a brief but emphatic verbal response followed by a quiet moment as you wait for the next question.

Now imagine the interview is being wound up. Getting up and picking your bag up while still talking or being watched can be a trickier manoeuvre than you might think. Lean forward in the start of a crouch, take the handle of your bag in one hand and steady yourself by placing the other on the arm of your chair. Then straighten up. Pause at full height (I've seen some candidates who never stand fully upright, staying in a semi-crouch while they're talking, like Groucho Marx).

Shake hands again, using the same skills of eye contact and your congruent-looking smile. Walk out.

Not all interview chairs are the bog-standard upright variety. Some interviewers prefer the more casual sofa-style seat. Although their intentions are good, it can be an interviewee's nightmare. Sofas tend to be lower than normal chairs and the seats longer. This means having to launch yourself downward and backward without really knowing where you're going to land. As with the normal chair, sit at the front first before pushing yourself in a small 'bottom-bob' to the back. Don't go too far – sprawling shouldn't be an option!

Unbutton your jacket. There will be advice on dress later in the book but while you're rehearsing do check to see whether your interview outfit works with you or against you. As you take your seat, flip your jacket button open so that you don't sit down looking too buttoned up and with your jacket shoulders rising up around your ears.

Check out your socks. Sometimes it's not until you cross your legs and take a look in the mirror that you realise you're 'shin-flashing', i.e. showing an expanse of bare flesh between the top of your sock and the hem of your trousers. Pop-sox are less popular for women but some still wear them with a skirt to interviews, flashing that very unattractive welt at the top as they cross their legs.

Check out your skirt. A skirt used to be appropriate formal wear for women in business but now it's entirely optional. Smart skirts are currently back in fashion, so more women are opting to wear them for job interviews. If you do – and especially if you normally live in jeans and combats – please rehearse a lot in your pencil skirt. Some are horrendously deceptive, hanging at a discreet knee-length when you're standing up but rising to reveal a vast chunk of thigh once you're sitting down.

Other skirts do it via a side or front vent, suddenly unfurling like a curtain in a peep-show to treat your interviewer to a chunk of prime cellulite, or there are those horrible back vents that are often cut right up to your bottom. It's easily possible to sport this 'back-flash' look without ever being aware of it, as most of us forget to take that all-important backward glance when we're looking in the mirror. Do check it out. I know they are vital for walking but they also tend to split a few stitches as we're getting onto the bus or into a taxi. A flash of your pants disappearing into the sunset is probably a bad signal when you're trying to be taken seriously for a new job.

Is there any other flesh baring or threatened flesh baring going on with your interview outfit? Do the buttons of your shirt pull apart and gap? Is your collar too tight? Does your tie go askew? Does your shirt lose contact with your waistband? Is flesh oozing anywhere? Are seams stretching to contain you? Are thongs or pant-tops suddenly visible above the water-line? If so, deal with it. Your outfit should both sit and stand gracefully without all these sartorial traumas upstaging you and spoiling the show.

Reading your interviewer's body language

Body language is a two-way process and while you're busy sending out all the right signals about yourself via your own body talk you should also be tapped into your interviewer's non-verbal communications.

This is much harder than adjusting your own gestures and expression. Why? Well, there are so many variables. However, it's still vital you remain perceptive even if you're remembering not to be overly judgemental.

Many body language guides suggest each gesture has one prime purpose. This means you may well believe that if someone touches their nose they are lying, or if they fold their arms they're feeling anxious. I wish it was that easy, if it were I'd be out in Las Vegas right now, cleaning up at the poker tables. The fact is that each gesture can have many meanings, some almost completely contradictory. Folding your arms, for instance, can mean defensiveness or aggression, depending on how it is performed.

When you're considering your own body language signals, it's important to focus on what they might appear to say to other people rather than how you actually feel as you do them. When you read other people's signals, you'll be hunting for the truth and that comes less from one gesture and more from **cluster signals**.

Cluster signals

Take a word out of a sentence and it can be difficult to define and the same is true of one gesture taken out of context. To get a more accurate view of someone else's thoughts and feelings you will need to evaluate the whole pose, balancing one gesture against another.

To explain in business terms: your interviewer begins your interview leaning forward and using eye contact, smiling and nods. At some point in the interview, she stops smiling and her eye contact moves towards the door. Is she:

- completely bored with you and wishing the interview would end?
- aware that a major fire has just broken out in the outer office?
- dying to go to the toilet?

To get closer to the truth you'd need to examine other evidence. Did she stop nodding as well? Has her body language become stressed or anxious? Have her eyes glazed over? Is she jiggling in her chair?

This scanning of the cluster signals might sound like a long and complex process but in fact your brain can do it in a matter of seconds. The key point is, then: **Be perceptive!** (but don't be too quick to diagnose).

Tune in as you talk. Place your brain and your faculties in what athletes and performers call **the zone** and what I call **the moment**. Be in the room with your thoughts, not wandering around in the car park. Be alert, sharp and focused. And – please – don't view your interviewer's body language signals through paranoia goggles. This means reading every gesture he or she uses in a negative way. Individual gestures or expressions can have several different meanings, so don't jump to the conclusion that a long look is a disapproving glare, or that glancing away means you're boring them. Both gestures could be signals of concentration!

The following symptoms are just a guide. Look out for them but then evaluate according to the interviewer's overall signals.

Signs that your interviewer is connected

- Genuine, symmetric smiling that reaches the eyes.
- Nodding that seems paced to your verbal delivery.
- Leaning forward.
- Slightly mirroring your body language, i.e. smiling when you do, moving into similar positions.
- Stillness: low body movement when you speak.
- No fiddling or fidgeting.

- Listening first, then writing notes.
- Open gestures.
- Use of a hand/arm gesture known as the **empty embrace**, i.e. holding both hands out towards you slightly, palms facing one another.

Signs that your interviewer has disconnected

- Rigid, fake smiling.
- Suppressed yawns.
- Doing something else while you talk, like doodling or reading through paperwork.
- Writing notes at the same time as you're speaking (this might appear as though they're taking down every word that falls out of your mouth, but being genuinely engaged means having a desire to watch the person speak as well as note down the essence of their words).
- Face-touching.
- Resting their chin in the palm of their hand.
- Taking calls.
- Sitting back and folding their arms.
- Pushing back from the table or desk.
- Turning their torso away at an angle.
- Gazing up and to their left.
- Stretching as if trying to wake up.
- Offering the wrong body language response, i.e. laughing when you've just told them about a problem you had with your last job.
- A sudden increase in self-comfort signals like hair-stroking, nail-picking or fiddling with jewellery.
- A sudden increase in impatient signals like jiggling or fidgeting, touching their watch or puffing.
- Placing both hands palm-down on the desk or table, especially if it's done with a flourish.
- Stacking or tidying their paperwork or packing it away.
- Metronomic gestures, i.e. tapping.

Possible disapproval gestures

- A brief eyebrow shrug, raised quickly and then dropped.
- Lip-pursing.
- Fingers under their chin with one finger placed up the side of the face.
- A sideways head-tilt i.e. a half head-shake.
- Frowning.

- Eye-narrowing.
- Mouth-shrug.
- Tongue-poke (a slight poking out of the tongue from the front of the mouth).
- Lower jaw-jutting.
- Or lower lip-jutting.
- Clenching of the teeth.
- Asymmetric smiling.
- Alerting signals, like an eye-flash (a quick but meaningful glance) or a raised finger.
- Accelerated blink rate.
- Cut-off signals, like a dropped head or eyes closing.
- Eye-blocks i.e. long, slow blinks.
- Eye-shuffle (looking quickly from side to side).
- Hand-swatting gestures, appearing to swat you away.
- Leg-clamping (placing one leg over the other and then clamping it with their hands).
- Lightning smiles (appearing and then gone in a flash).

What to do if you believe you're turning them off

If you detect a change in mood during your interview and believe that may be down to something you did or said, try to avoid focusing on the past few moments, as over-analysing will mean you are in danger of scuppering the present. There are two key questions that you need to examine quickly:

1. Did the interviewer's attitude change while you were talking? If so, what was it you said that might have turned them off?
2. Sometimes an interviewer will make his or her feelings felt very clearly if they are unhappy with your response. This is likely to have verbal affirmations as well, as in 'Oh really?' 'Do you?' 'Is that all?'

Try to keep calm – panic, no matter how mild, won't help you regain lost ground.

Ask yourself if it's a bad thing that you have been controversial. Are you applying for a job that will involve you challenging existing processes and behaviours? Not every job interviewer is looking for a 'yes' man or woman.

One thing can make the situation worse and that's trying to wriggle out of what you've said. If you've offered an opinion and done so very forcefully it could make you look insincere if you suddenly change that opinion just because you feel they don't agree with you. One company I worked with used to question applicants on their daily newspaper. Whatever the applicant said the interviewer would look shocked and slightly disgusted: 'The Times? You read *The Times?*'

Or they might ask a question about a basic opinion 'Do you think recycling should be the job of government or individuals?' Again, whatever answer was given would register obvious disapproval. Over half the applicants would back down immediately, believing they'd made a mistake. But by trying to correct their mistake they only placed themselves lower down the ladder in terms of chances of getting the job, as the company would see them as sycophantic and untrustworthy.

Always avoid using flustered or defensive body language. Don't suddenly cross your arms in a body-barrier or become visually agitated. Try to maintain the same pose that you used when you made your comment, but pause to judge their response and hear what they have to say. If necessary, go some way to explain your opinions further but don't waffle when you do. Once your body language rhythms and patterns of movement start to deteriorate it can be difficult to regain your composure.

TEN EASY WAYS TO CREATE A BAD IMPRESSION

10

- Sweaty handshake
- No eye contact
- Chewing gum
- Shrugging when asked a question
- Laughing at inappropriate moments
- Getting the name of the company or its product wrong
- Wearing unpolished shoes
- Making your first question about money or a pay rise
- Saying 'yeah' instead of 'yes'
- Leaving your phone on.

TEN EASY WAYS TO CREATE A GOOD IMPRESSION

10

- Give a nice firm, dry handshake
- Look your interviewer/s in the eye, especially when you're listening to them
- Smile at all the right moments
- Look keen and energetic
- Show you have knowledge of the job, company and product or service
- Wear polished (but not brand new) shoes
- Use emphatic hand gestures to show the right emotion at the right time
- Be congruent – ensure your words, tone of voice and gestures all give out the same message
- Mirror their body language – subtly!
- Thank them before you leave and touch them again – but only with a handshake!

IN A NUTSHELL

- Be aware of your own first impressions: your interviewer will have started to assess you as soon as you walk into the room.
- Work on your etiquette: give good handshakes and greetings and learn how to do the room at networking events.
- Use body language techniques like mirroring to create rapport.
- Link in to their communication style to create stronger bonding and understanding.

7 HOW TO DRESS THE PART

In this chapter, you'll find out everything about dressing right for your interviews, from your choice of suit to the colour of your tie or the size of your bag. Tips and techniques will include:

- how to choose the right outfit for the right job
- what 'smart/casual' really means
- picking the appropriate accessories
- how colours can effect the interviewer's perception of your personality and mood.

Why smart means safe

The ideal choice of interview outfit is probably a lot less random than you think. Although fashion provides multiple variations of style, cut and colour only a small percentage of companies take advantage of this freedom of expression, and only a smaller percent of that percentage would be happy to see anything other than classic formal wear during a recruitment interview.

HOW TO LOOK WEIRD

There's nothing wrong with individuality or even eccentricity (if there was I'd be in big trouble!) but an interview isn't the ideal time to air the edgier side of your personality. Conformity might sound dull but for most interviewers it also sounds 'safe'. Remember, they're hoping to introduce you to and integrate you with the rest of their workforce/customers, so pack up the 'I'm a bit of a character, me!' stuff and try to look humanoid for a couple of hours at least.

Ditch any or all of the following:

- badges
- cat jewellery
- body piercing (ear piercings are ok though!) or tattoos unless you're applying for a job at a tattoo parlour
- punctuating all your statements with abrupt, nervous laughter
- sniffing
- biting your nails while you're talking
- staring
- showing too much flesh, i.e. cleavage or leg
- piling more than two sugars into your tea or coffee
- eating more than one biscuit (if offered)
- keeping glancing at the clock
- a chewed biro
- plastic carrier bag
- cartoon socks or ties

- eyeshadow matching your outfit
- a hat
- long false nails
- your *Psycho* ringtone
- clogs
- your name on a necklace (or anywhere, really)
- underpants visible above trousers
- glitter
- high fashion, unless you're applying for a job at *Vogue*
- a pocket hankie
- bow tie or cravat
- a belt with a large buckle, especially a death's head
- drop earrings
- satin (apart from a blouse)
- florals
- coloured tights
- cowboy boots.

Looking smart and dressing smart have psychological implications that exceed what might be a company's normal dress code. You could consider taking risks with your outfit in a bid to register individuality and self-expression, but that's rarely what a business is looking for. Very few interviewers are risk-takers, with most just wanting the closest fit to the job vacancy.

One IT graduate wore a suit and tie to his first interview, only to discover the entire firm was emphatically casual. He slipped off his tie and opened the neck of his shirt but was told during his post-interview feedback that they'd appreciated his keenness at arriving more formally dressed.

One girl applying for a place at art college to study textile design was told she had nearly been turned down because she wore a pencil skirt and smart shirt, which they thought wasn't artistic enough for their college.

She arrived at her next college dressed in jeans and a parka, only to find the interviewer sitting in front of her in a three-piece suit and bow tie.

The messages you'll be sending out via your choice of outfit will be:

- **etiquette:** a smart, formal suit lets the company know you have respect and view your interview with a sense of occasion
- **status:** smarter clothes imply higher status
- **self-esteem:** there are strong links between a smart, well-groomed look and confidence and self-worth
- **group integration:** by dressing like the group or pack you want to join, you help them to see you as a potential member
- **your personality:** that tie could be more telling than you think!
- **your mood:** top-to-toe beige or grey might suggest depression.

So dressing appropriately is vital. The only time you should risk pushing the boat out in terms of more fashionable or controversial gear is if:

- you know for sure that the business or company you are applying to holds exceptionally creative and off-the-wall thinkers in such high esteem that they are prepared to rock and roll with whatever you decide to shrug yourself into
- you're applying for a job as a presenter on children's TV
- you know they're utterly desperate to fill the vacancy and have no other applicants
- you don't really want the job
- you're the son/daughter of the owner of the company.

Grooming

This is an area that should be risk free – your well-groomed appearance sends out vital signals of appropriateness and respect for the occasion. The following checklist might appear to be stating the obvious but – as most interviewers have their horror stories – please work through it anyway!

General tips

These apply to both men and women.

- Always take a bath or shower on the morning of your interview.
- Apply a good antiperspirant deodorant, unperfumed if possible.
- Don't imagine that perfume or cologne do the same job.
- Avoid sprays that leave white marks, especially if you're wearing a dark-coloured outfit.

- If you have a problem with foot odour, use a good foot spray.
- And possibly pop some charcoal insoles into your interview shoes.
- Shoes retain smells. Even if your feet are clean, the heat from them could trigger bad odours, especially if your shoes are made of rubber or plastic.
- Make sure your hair is freshly washed. Day-old hair might look clean but it absorbs smells like cooking, smoke or from travelling on the underground.
- If you gel, use a light touch with the products. Over-gelled hair looks tacky.
- Invest in a good, easy-to-manage haircut just before your interview.
- Avoid eating foods with garlic or onion the day before your interview and take breath fresheners just in case.
- Make sure your nails look impeccably manicured. Clean them thoroughly, using a wooden manicure stick to clean out any deeper dirt and cut and file them to a neat shape.
- If you chew your nails, make an extra effort to stop before your interviews, as bitten nails can imply anxiety. Try paint-on or bitter-tasting products from the chemist or even wear cotton gloves at times when you know you often tend to get stuck in.
- If you have a cold or hayfever, explain and apologise and keep a hankie handy – never sit sniffing!
- Never turn up sporting nicotine-stained fingers.
- Make sure your interview outfit is freshly washed or dry-cleaned and pressed. If you have a long journey take your jacket with you in a suit bag and hang it either in the back of your car or over your arm if you're using public transport. Never arrive looking crumpled.
- Take a small, traveller's sewing kit in case buttons drop off or hems start to fall down …
- … and a travelling clothes brush.
- Make sure your shoes are clean, well polished and in a good state of repair.

For men!

- Avoid wearing nylon socks.
- Trim nasal and ear hairs.
- Make sure you look clean shaven. If your beard is heavy and your interview is at the end of the day take a battery shaver with you so you can shave before you get there.
- Only wear light, lemony colognes and never over-apply, as it's possible to become immune to the smell when you've had it on for a couple of hours.

- Remove any piercings.
- Take a spare tie in case you drop food or spill drink down the one you're wearing.

For women!

- If you're wearing tights, take a spare pair.
- Keep jewellery to a minimum and wear nothing that makes a noise, like a charm bracelet.
- Avoid heady or sickly perfumes.
- Don't overdo the make-up: a light, natural look is best.
- Avoid long nail extensions and any form of nail art.
- Avoid strong-coloured varnishes: neutral is best but not French manicure.
- Avoid elaborate hair accessories.
- If you have long hair, do think about tying it back or pinning it up.

Styling

General

The suit should be a lightweight wool rather than thick or chunky and it will help if you can buy a fabric with plenty of drape, i.e. movement. Some business suits tend to be made of rather stiff fabrics that are ungainly to wear.

Always check for the crumple factor before you buy. Crush some of the fabric up in your hand, hold for a few seconds, then release. Is it creased? If so, don't buy it.

Linen is a fabulous fabric for summer but you should avoid buying a linen or linen-blend suit for interviews.

If you're buying a jacket or a suit, look at the seams before you buy. There should be no wrinkling or pulling around the seams, so check out as many as they have in your size and try to pick the most well-made, wrinkle-free one.

Only ever iron suit fabrics through a clean cloth, never place the iron directly onto the fabric.

When you're buying your suit, pay careful attention to size. An expensive suit will look cheap if it's too tight, but a cheap suit can look more expensive if it fits well. Make sure the buttons do up easily, without pulling and never buy a jacket in a smaller size with the intention of wearing it open.

Check shoulder width and waist size. Your sleeves should be no longer than just touching the 'heel' of the hand and your trousers should have just one 'break' or indent before they hit the shoe. Too short and you'll look as if you've outgrown your clothes; too long will make you look as if you're on your first day at junior school!

Try to keep all your pockets empty for an interview. Men tend to use their clothes as carrier bags but this spoils the lines of the outfit, making it look baggy rather than smart.

Empty pens out of breast pockets and phones, hankies, money and anything else out of trouser and jacket pockets. Most women's suits are bought with the pockets stitched up and it's a good idea to keep them this way.

Men

Men wearing a single-breasted jacket should do up the middle button but undo it before they sit down.

A double-breasted jacket should always be buttoned up.

High-buttoned jackets are currently popular for men, with four buttons or even more at the front. If you're buying one of these for an interview, check how easily you will be able to slip the buttons open before you sit down.

Men's waistcoats are currently less popular but if they do make a return always remember to keep the bottom button open.

A plain, well-ironed shirt is ideal.

Cuffs should reach the heel of the hand and cufflinks can look great for an immaculate, formal, work-wear look, but only with turn-back cuffs.

Women

A smart trouser or skirt suit is the classic interview outfit, although a jacket and skirt or trousers is suitable smart wear for women.

Plain fabrics are better than any with a large design, like a check or spot. Busy patterns can be upstaging and you want to keep the attention on you.

Avoid floral prints, as they look non-professional and possibly wedding-y.

Shiny fabrics like satin only work for an evening outfit; do make sure you don't create an unintentionally shiny look by ironing your suit on the outside!

If you're wearing a shorter jacket, do check that your trousers or skirt fit perfectly. Well-tailored and well-cut women's trousers are hard to find, but an unflattering shape or fit can look horrible without a longer jacket to cover the bum and thighs.

A skirt needs to be knee-length, even if the fashion is to wear them shorter or longer.

The length of your jacket should be determined by your height. Taller women can take a longer jacket (single or double-breasted, according to fashion) but look odd in anything shorter or cropped to the waist. Short women need a neater length and single-breast fastening.

Trouser turn-ups have made a bit of a comeback for women rather than men. Fluff tends to collect in them and I do remember watching one applicant cross her legs confidently, only to find a lump of grey fluff plopping out in front of the interviewers!

Cardigans are also currently going through a 'cool' revival. They look great as a fashion item but unfortunately still look a bit 'granny' for an interview.

A simple, round-necked top is better than a shirt when you're wearing it under a jacket. I rarely recommend shirts for women underneath a jacket as we don't wear ties, meaning the open shirt collar can slide all over the place, looking scruffy.

Alternative smart wear for women would be a plain, well-cut dress or a smart shirt tucked into trousers or a skirt.

Coat dresses work well, as do sleeveless, knee-length black dresses worn under full-length or shorter jackets.

Colours

If you're buying an interview suit, it's best to stick within the business spectrum, which means navy, grey, charcoal or black for your basic colours (suits for men, dresses, trousers or skirts for women). Women can wear a variety of other colours but I'd advise against buying a whole suit in bright colours like red, pink or blue; team a brighter jacket with your basic colour skirt or trousers.

For a man the safest shirt colours are white or a chambray (light) blue. For a woman choosing the top to wear under the jacket I'd suggest holding the fabric up under your chin and looking in a mirror to see how it either flatters or drains your skin tone.

There is something to be said for colour psychology, i.e. not just wearing colours that suit your flesh and hair tones but also selecting them to create a kind of clothing ambience. For business this will be even more important than for social wear. It's sometimes touted as a complex science but here's a more speedy, down-to-earth guide for your interview charisma.

- **Black:** a solid business choice for skirts and trousers or even suits for women but it can look a little funereal for men. Avoid wearing too much black, i.e. make sure it's matched with a contrasting tone to bring your outfit to life. White or cream are best. Beware – cheap black fabrics don't take black dye so well and it can emerge as an 'off-black', so if you're working on a budget, black might not be the best choice. Black also shows up flecks and dust so dandruff sufferers might like to choose a safer colour.
- **Navy:** possibly the safest business colour as it implies integrity and professionalism and is one of the most flattering colours to every skin tone, even if it does feel a bit boring to wear.
- **Charcoal:** a high-status business colour. Again, flattering to most skin tones, especially with a crisp white shirt or top.
- **Grey:** a paler grey can look dreary and imply a boring character. Unless you have a tan this can also be draining.
- **Yellow:** creative, energetic, positive and keen. Not so committed to logical or strategic thinking. Use it sparingly, like a tie for men, or jacket or shirt for women.
- **Red:** this colour excites the nervous system, so is seen as the colour of love but also anger! Red is a very dominant colour but a classic for ties and jackets for women.

- **Pink:** pink is the colour of sex! It's also a very 'girlie' choice, beloved by topless celebs etc. Pink shirts for men swing in and out of popularity at an alarming rate. Bright pink can look attention-seeking and baby pink ... well, babyish!
- **Blue:** the colour of calm and empathy. A good 'mixing' colour.
- **Brown:** seen as a rather dull, traditional colour with overtones of country life. Still rarely seen in the City, where brown shoes or suits can cause grown men to faint with horror!
- **Green:** a softer, more approachable colour that is now strongly linked with environmental issues. Not the most flattering colour for many skin tones, as it can reflect up into the face, projecting a look of nausea!
- **Orange:** this colour has often been chosen to create a positive, happy ambience in restaurants and cafés, but wearing it as an interview choice can be risky. Burnt orange is safer than the lairy shades, which would imply original thinking and an extrovert personality.
- **Peacock:** a good 'bright' choice, as it has a enough blue in it to be both loud and serious at the same time.
- **Purple:** a high-status colour that is also quite calming and usually flattering as a deeper tone.
- **White:** clean, smart, with nothing to hide.
- **Beige:** can imply an insipid personality, especially if worn top to toe.
- **Caramel:** a richer tone that will imply more personality and confidence than beige.

Accessories

Ties are the most expressive part of a man's business dress and it's important to choose carefully. Avoid amusing ties with animal pictures or 'funny' prints. A striped tie can look smart but a bit 'school uniform' if you happen to be young. Anything too loud or busy might be distracting, but there are some great brightly coloured ties currently on sale, so you needn't pick the very boring option.

When you buy your tie, hold it by the narrow end and let it drop to see if it twists as it hangs. If it does, it might be a problem to wear, as it's possibly been stitched badly.

Always button the top button of your shirt collar and make sure your tie knot fits snugly into it. If your ties tend to go walkabout you could invest in a plain, subtle tiepin to keep it in place and to avoid the narrow end showing.

When you tie your tie, the proper length should be just touching or just covering your belt. Never wear it with a gap between tie and belt and never tuck it into your belt!

If you're wearing cufflinks, they should be very plain. Classic, oval gold links are always OK, and other plain styles will work, even in colours. Avoid 'funny cuffs' like cars, pigs, tap-heads or football logos.

Socks should be plain and ideally black. Buy longer socks to avoid shin-flashing as you sit down. No logos, cartoons, checks or spots etc and no bright colours like red or yellow!

The safest shoe for men is a classic lace-up in black leather, either plain or brogue. The soles should be thin leather, not thick and rubbery, and avoid current fashion looks like chisel or pointed toes.

For women a classic court shoe is safest and no boots unless you wear ankle boots under trousers. Only ever wear higher heels if you're confident you can walk well in them and absolutely no killer heels!

A simple chain or necklace can look smart with a plain neckline but avoid brooches and scarves as they tend to be very ageing.

A briefcase is the ultimate business bag, although you won't be expected to carry one if this is your first job. Never walk in lugging carrier bags or pull-alongs. If you're staying overnight ask if you can leave bigger bags in reception.

You might be called on to open your briefcase during your interview to recover documents or an extra copy of your CV. Keep contents neat and practical. I once opened mine and a half-eaten chocolate bar and a celebrity magazine slid out onto the floor! I always remember one applicant who – for some reason – had squashed a sliced loaf into her briefcase!

Handbags need to be selected for their manageability. If it's a shoulder bag will it stay on your shoulder easily? Avoid bags that need to be over-clutched, as you shouldn't walk in with your arm crossing your body to clasp at your bag strap. Classic, queen-style handbags will look a bit stuffy and Margaret

Thatcher-ish; make sure a smaller, handle-free purse doesn't fall out from under your arm as you go to shake hands.

Do invest in a nice-looking pen. Old biros or freebie logo pens don't look as good as a smart felt-tip or something that looks quality.

Although you're likely to shuck your coat off in reception, it's important to arrive wearing a nice businesslike coat over your suit. Anoraks don't work and neither does other sportswear. Avoid anything fur or fleece-lined, as the fluff might end up all over your nice dark jacket.

IN A NUTSHELL

- Choose your outfit carefully and err on the side of caution regarding smart and casual wear. Most interviews are still seen as formal occasions.
- Make sure your grooming is immaculate. Scruffy shoes will often emerge at the top of most interviewer's no-go lists.
- Take the right accessories. Remember the saying 'The devil is in the detail' – no nasty cheap pens or inappropriate bags or cases.

8 HOW TO TALK THE TALK

In Chapter 11 I will be giving you advice about your answers to interview questions. However, your verbal input at interview stage isn't just about coming up with smart answers. In this chapter, we'll be looking at four very powerful aspects of speech:

- your vocal tone and projection
- psycholinguistics: choosing the right words at the right time
- red rag words and phrases
- making small talk before the actual interview begins.

You and your words

You've probably been talking since you were two, but not the kind of talking that helps get jobs. An interview involves what I call **performance talking**, where every word counts. Worried? You should be! However, achieving verbal excellence is relatively easy and this chapter will explain exactly all you need to know to achieve it.

Your listening skills

It might seem strange to start a chapter on speaking with a section on listening but the first skill of communication is active listening. When you learn to listen properly, you learn to understand. And once you've understood, your own responses will be 20 times more effective.

Several things can create poor listening:

- nerves or anxiety
- distractions
- boredom
- language or accent problems
- background noise
- assumptions (you assume your already know what they're telling you)
- poor communication skills from the speaker.

Being 'in the room'

To be an effective listener you will need to be focused, or what psychologists often call 'in the room'. Your brain is like a bird, flying backwards and forwards rather than sitting for long on one spot, and you will need to take control over your thinking and concentration.

Your mind has three key sites that it likes to visit: the past, the present and the future. Out of those three, our brains will spend longer dwelling on the past and future and very little time in the here and now. We daydream, we worry, we go over what we just said, we think ahead to how it will feel to get turned down, we imagine what the interviewer might be thinking and what he or she's going to say next. All of this dilutes our ability to stay fiercely in the present, hanging on every word that we're being told.

Listening techniques

There are six key skills for effective and active listening and you should aim to use all of them during your interviews:

1. don't interrupt
2. pause to consider the question before you supply the answer
3. never assume you know what they're going to say
4. avoid 'queuing', i.e. thinking of all your answers while the other person is still speaking
5. ask for clarification to check you've got the point
6. use the **reflecting technique** to scorch the question into your brain: 'you want to know about my management experience ... well ...' but don't answer every question in this way.

Talk saves lives

How good are your basic communication skills? Here's a quick checklist – how many of these statements do you agree with?

- I do most of my business communications via email.
- I do most of my social communications via text.
- I often text or work online while colleagues are talking to me. I'm a pretty good multi-tasker.
- I'm fine talking to friends but more hesitant talking to strangers in business.
- I'm a quiet person by nature.
- I hate being looked at while I talk.
- I've taken time off work and during that time I only really communicated with my children during the day.
- I spent any spare time when I was off work communicating online.
- This is my first job. My only real communications have been with mates and other students.
- I'm OK when I get to know people.
- When I get nervous I tend to talk too much.
- When I get nervous I tend to talk too little.
- When I get nervous I talk too quickly and start tripping over my words.
- I tend to allow my voice to trail off at the end of sentences.
- I use too many 'ums' and 'ers' or 'you knows' and this gets worse when I'm under pressure.

- I often hear myself answering a different question from the one I was asked, or straying off the point.
- My voice tends to get higher in pitch when I get nervous.
- I often find myself clearing my throat a lot when I'm nervous.
- I'm not good at explaining myself.
- I'm not always a very tactful person – I tend to speak my mind.

How many did you agree with? The score is unimportant, although the more items you agree with, the more work you need to be doing on your communication and interpersonal skills. Even one item needs attention, though. Any or all of the above statements could scupper your success at interview level.

Getting the tone right

Nervousness, stress and anxiety can all have a negative effect on your voice, leading to vocal quavering, a higher pitch, a breathless delivery, stammering or the kind of staccato monotone that makes you sound like a Dalek! There are some simple steps you can take to prevent all this from happening.

Breathe out

Have you ever been told to take a deep breath to calm yourself down? The problem with this piece of advice is that inhaling tenses the muscles and wires the brain. It's the *out*-breath you need to focus on to relax those vocal chords and drop your vocal tone a note or two. I've already given tips on your breathing to calm yourself down (see page 000) and the great news is that all those exercises will have a fantastic effect on your voice, too.

Count your own rhythm

When a singer starts to sing, he or she will often count themselves in, counting off a few beats to act as a personal metronome. You can act as your own mini-metronome when you start to speak, too. Take a small pause and count yourself in at the ideal pace. If you find your pace and tone go wrong as you start to gather speed you can always use a very subtle physical metronomic gesture to supply that ideal pace throughout your communication. A small tapping of the foot or finger should act subliminally but make sure it can't be seen or it could signal impatience or anxiety to your interviewer.

Sipping water

You'll probably be offered a drink during your interview and still water will be the best choice for your voice. Sip it rather than glugging it down. Alternatively, you could find a mint or throat sweet will appear to relax your vocal chords a bit. No chewing gum, as you might forget to take it out before you go in – and do try to avoid strongly coloured throat sweets. You don't want to sit talking with a cherry-red or orange-coloured tongue!

Give your voice a work-out

Ideal pre-interview preparation would be to try reading out loud. If you're not used to speaking to strangers in formal situations, you could find you tend to mumble or speak too quietly. Most of us have a **verbal shorthand** we use when we talk to friends, colleagues and family and this involves a lot of colloquialisms, incomplete sentences and sloppy diction or pronunciation. Your vocal tone could also be rather flat, so try these two easy activities and keep doing them right up until your interview:

ACTIVITY 4

FOCUS ON WORDS

Take this list of words and read them out loud, pausing between each word. Pronounce the entire word, exaggerating your pronunciation where possible. Alongside each word, I have written how it should sound when you say it. This exercise will help to make you realise how unclear your speech can normally be. Often we communicate with grunts, slang and half-finished dialogue. Hear and feel the difference when you pronounce them normally and then clearly:

Kickback	(pronouncing each 'k')
Problem	(pronouncing the 'e' clearly)
Hospital	(making the 't-a-l' clear)
Asking	(getting the first three letters in the right order: 'a-s-k')
Million	(pronouncing both 'i's)
Different	(pronouncing both 'e's, not 'diffrnt')
Influenza	(all four syllables!)
Interview	(all three syllables!)
Squirrel	(making the 'e' clear)
Sickening	(making the 'e' clear)

Reading out loud is like a gym workout for the body, it airs your vocal cords and works all the mouth muscles that might normally be suffering from neglect. Take a children's book with lots of action sequences, stand at one end of a room and read to the other end, making it as entertaining and exciting as possible. Exaggerate your diction so that every syllable is clear. Over-act and over-exaggerate and project your voice as you do so. This technique will teach you to achieve a natural-sounding rise and fall in your voice, plus **pointing** – using an amphatic tone to add meaning to your speech. Pointing is the verbal equivalent of using italics when you're writing or typing.

ACTIVITY 5

GIVE MEANING TO YOUR WORDS

Write down the following phrase on an A4 sheet of paper, then pin it or lean it up in front of you.

'Did you give Mark the book yesterday?'
Read the sentence out loud eight times, the first time in a monotone. Each of the remaining seven times you should add emphasis by verbally pointing to each word in the sentence at a time, i.e:

- DID you give Mark the book yesterday?
- Did YOU give Mark the book yesterday?
- Did you GIVE Mark the book yesterday? ... and so on.

This is an exercise in the power of your vocal tone and how necessary it is to give meaning to your words. Each time you say this sentence it will have a different meaning. Listen to how your vocal tone has to curve upward at the end to turn a sentence into a question.

When you repeat this sentence, make sure you keep your body still, making your vocal tone do all the work. Often we add emphasis via head nods, eyebrow raises or even body baton gestures. Although you can add these during real speech, this exercise will be more effective if you can train your voice to do all the work by itself.

Use these tips from the acting profession:

- Take a piece of writing, like a newspaper article
- Use a highlighter pen to underline all the words in that article that you would place vocal emphasis on and use pointing to give the passage meaning
- Read it out loud, using the highlighter to help you point to all the right words with your tone alone.

Projectile words

Learning to project doesn't mean learning to shout, it means making sure your voice is heard easily and that your tone sounds normal. A soft or quiet vocal tone isn't necessarily a bad thing as long as it is audible but if the interviewers have trouble hearing what you say, you will need to take steps to power your voice up.

Voice projection can be improved with some simple exercises. Your lungs are like the bellows of your voice, so breathing correctly is important. An actor projects by powering his or her voice from the diaphragm and lower lung, but when you get tense or feel under pressure your breathing will become shallower, rather than deeper and louder. This makes your voice sound weak, breathless and possibly tremulous.

ACTIVITY 6

DIRECT YOUR VOICE

Stand up straight with both feet planted firmly on the ground. Pull your spine up to full height and let your arms hang loosely down at your sides. Breathe in a good lungful of air and allow your lower lung to expand as you do. Remember your voice is going to come from your diaphragm, not your chest or your throat. Try repeating the word 'ACTOR' over and over again, propelling the word across the room with the power of your lungs. Relax as you do this. Avoid any tension in your neck, shoulder or throat muscles but do try to drop your voice to a few notes lower than usual, even if it sounds unnaturally deep as a result.

When you've done this a few times, pick out an object in the room, the further away from you the better. You're going to aim and direct your voice towards that object, visualising it 'hitting' the object as you say its name. This technique should feel as although the word is being fired out of your mouth like an arrow. By visualising its path and goal, you'll be able to control tone and distance quite easily. It helps if you sound rather angry as you say its name, i.e:

- 'CHAIR!'
- 'PICTURE!'
- 'WINDOW!'

When you project the word in this way, try to imagine whether you 'hit' the object or not. Did it feel as if it fell short? If so, try again and keep trying until you feel your voice is 'hitting' the object. If you're struggling, try pointing to the object as you say its name.

Psycholinguistics: the power of your words

Let's begin by having a very brief look at the process of speech.

- You get an idea, image or emotion in your mind.
- You process that 'thought bubble' into words (making you the encoder).
- You quickly assess or filter those words.
- You speak them out loud.
- Your listener translates your words into images and thoughts (making them the decoder).
- Your listener stores those thoughts away in his or her head.

Much of what we hear will be misinterpreted. Have you ever brought up a row at home and been told: 'That's not what I said' or 'That's not what I meant'?

You need to choose your words carefully in any communication, but especially an important communication with what could be complete strangers, like a job interview.

Negative marketing

It's important that your interview dialogues hit the right spot between sounding negative and sounding arrogant or boastful.

We'll look at some specific questions in Chapter 11, but here are some examples of how easy it is to veer to either extreme and create a bad impression in the process:

- **Interviewer:** Do you have any experience in sales?
- **You:** Not really, just a holiday job when I was at school (under-sell)
- **Or:** Yes I'm brilliant at sales. I can sell anything to anyone (over-sell)
- **Or:** Yes, in fact I took a part-time retail job to ensure I had some experience (spot-on).

Negative words and under-sell terms include:

- only
- just I hope
- this job would be a challenge for me
- quite
- not bad at
- I'd be prepared to have a go
- my friends/family are always telling me I'm quite good
- I got bored at home
- I haven't really thought about it
- I don't know
- my husband/wife said I should give it a try
- I think I could cope
- it might be a laugh
- I'm sorry
- I suppose so
- I might be all right
- I'd try.

Over-sell words include:

- fantastic
- I'm the best
- I guarantee you won't regret it

- I'll give 200%
- I'm really, really good
- I'm known to be top in that
- I never fail
- Fail isn't an option
- if you don't give me this job today I shall keep coming back until you do
- I know I can do this job better than any of the other candidates
- I'm successful in everything I turn my hand at
- I'm a winner, not a loser
- I want to be doing your job in under a year
- if you don't give this job to me I shall go to a rival company instead
- I've had lots of offers
- I don't need to work
- I had my own multi-million pound company but decided I would be happier working for other people. Who needs all that hassle?
- the other company knew I was too good for them. They got me out before I quit
- they were jealous of my success
- the boss there knew I was better than she was and felt threatened by me.

Verbal fillers and how to avoid them!

What are verbal fillers? They're the noises, words and even short phrases you put into your speech to fill up gaps. When you get nervous, your use of fillers will increase. I've seen some interview candidates who manage to speak without adding any genuine conversation or information words in between all their fillers! Some of the most common fillers are:

- um …
- er …
- basically …
- actually …
- you know …
- sort of …
- kind of …
- like …
- innit?
- if you like …

Recognise them? You probably know your own particular favourite. Rumour has it one recent Prime Minister had a problem with the filler word 'actually', using it too frequently, especially when he was placed under pressure. During Prime Minister's question time in the House of Commons he'd struggle to avoid using it but the Opposition got wind of this and started to jeer every time it popped out of his mouth. This increased his inner negative command to 'stop using that word', which in turn increased his use of it, much to the delight of the Opposition!

As with unwanted body language gestures, the correct way to train your brain to delete these words from your repertoire is to focus on a better way to deal with your pauses. And the best way to deal with a pause is to do nothing – allow the pause to occur. Small silences allow you thinking time and allow your audience time to digest what you've just said. A silence or pause in a business conversation is not the same as a pause during a social conversation.

Social chats tend to be livelier and fast-paced but a business communication is normally riddled with brief pauses for emphasis and to aid understanding. Practise putting small pauses into your speech, at the end of each point and rehearse the use of confident body language signals as you do so. Clutching at your chest, rolling your eyes or fiddling will all signal the pause has occurred because you've lost your train of thought but good eye contact and a relaxed facial expression will imply the pause is intentional.

Slang and jargon

You might need to do work to 'pretty up' your language before you attend your interview. Why? Well, everyone has their own form of slang, shorthand or colloquialisms. These might work great when you're with people who speak the same shorthand, but will be meaningless to anyone else, much like text shorthand.

There is also a form of verbal etiquette during interviews and it's possible to sound rude without meaning to. Try to ensure you keep the following rules in mind:

- say 'yes' instead of 'yeah'
- never start an answer with the word 'obviously' – it implies the question was stupid

- never swear, even the mildest swearing and even if you apologise before or after
- never use the word 'whatever' – it sounds as though you have attitude
- say 'I'm sorry?', 'pardon' or 'would you mind repeating that?' if you don't hear a question, not 'what?' 'you what?' or 'eh?'
- always say 'thank you' if you're given tea or coffee or at the end of the interview. It's also good to thank the receptionist as you walk past on your way in.

Business jargon

How can I describe the utter horribleness of these terms? Business jargon is only marginally OK if it's technical terms and abbreviations. If you use these, you will need to remember that the interviewers might have no idea what you're talking about. They will only impress at an interview if they have genuine meaning for your audience. If there's a risk they won't, either don't use them or explain tactfully as you go, e.g: 'ISDI 2012 which, as you probably know, stands for ...'

But then there is cliché jargon, i.e. terms and phrases that someone rather sad made up and which go round business like the worst kind of virus. They might be funny or even smart for approximately 15 minutes but after that they're as stale as last night's take-away. A whole book could be dedicated to these phrases (and very likely has!) but here are some examples of the kind of thing I'm talking about. Please omit all traces of them from your communication during interviews:

- blue-sky thinking
- like trying to nail a jelly to the wall
- we'll run that one up the flagpole and see who salutes
- we're all singing from the same hymn sheet
- I'm on a learning curve
- cherry-picking jobs
- sexing it up
- moving the goalposts
- joined-up thinking
- down-sizing
- job upgrade
- I really nailed it

- that's right on the money
- the bigger picture.

Red rag words

There are some words or phrases that are almost guaranteed to annoy an interviewer. These are called **red rag** words and they can be used unwittingly. Here are some examples of the most commonly used ones.

- 'Why?' Used at the start of a question this word can sound judgemental and argumentative, e.g. 'Why do you want to know that?' or 'Why is that relevant?'
- 'I don't mean to be rude ...' This announces the fact you **are** about to be rude. Putting this at the start doesn't negate the rudeness in any way!
- 'I'm not being funny ...' Ditto.
- 'With respect ...' Ditto.
- 'You've got to ...', 'You should ...', 'You must ...', 'You have to ...', 'You ought to ...' These are all 'Ordering' or 'Tell' words and will appear to challenge your interviewer's status and authority. Saying 'You have to consider me for this post' or 'You've got to give me a try' might be guaranteed to do the exact opposite!
- 'Stupid'. There's no way to smuggle this into a sentence without sounding as if you're aiming it at the interviewer. 'That's a stupid idea', 'That's almost as stupid as my last job ...'
- 'No'. As a stand-alone this word sounds unhelpful and rude. 'Do you have any experience of this type of work?' 'No.' The phrase that will hang in the air is: 'and I don't want to, either'. Add positive words to avoid the bald 'No', such as: 'No I don't have any direct experience but I'm keen to do some training to make up for that'.
- 'I don't mind.' Phrases like this sound indifferent.
- 'Quite', as in 'I'm quite keen to work here' or 'I'm quite good at my job.' It's much too half hearted.

Structured speech

Although the overall control of your interview will be in the hands of the interviewer or interviewers themselves, there's nothing stopping you doing a little forward planning and structuring. This means getting your thoughts and ideas into some form of order that will nearly always be useable, even though you can never guarantee the type of questions you'll be asked.

This verbal structuring is called **widthways planning** and it involves taking a large sheet of paper, which you should turn horizontally and divide into four vertical columns. Label your columns as follows:

A: aims and objectives. This should be easy to fill because it will likely be something along the lines of 'Getting the job or promotion'.

L: limits. This is where you consider all the limitations of your interview, such as limited time, limited knowledge of you, possible use of jargon.

P: persuading and discussing. Write down all the key points that should persuade the interviewer to give you this job. Hone them to the job and company and remember to include proof, not just opinion. List your relevant qualities, experience and skills and then evidence, such as certificates, grades and actual experiences.

O: objections. Write down why you might not be right for the job. Where are you weak on qualifications or experience? Why might the interviewer have concerns about employing you this time? It's always a good idea to have an educated but objective evaluation of potential trouble spots like this. Once you're aware of any objections, you have the option of bringing them up yourself rather than waiting for them to emerge, or to at least have an answer ready should they pop up on their own. The following may be assertive ways of introducing them.

- I know I'm younger than most of the candidates and have less experience but I'm also very willing to learn and can bring a lot of fresh enthusiasm and energy to the job.
- I do understand this job would mean a cut in pay but I hope that proves how keen I am to get it.
- I know this job requires a driving licence, but I'm currently taking lessons and will have taken my test before the starting date. I've checked journey details and I could easily manage on public transport initially.

Making small talk

Whatever type of interview you're attending the style or stages of talking will probably go like this:

- very small small talk (e.g. 'How was your journey?')
- small talk (the chit-chat that breaks the ice)
- getting down to business (your interview questions)
- their talk (they tell you about the company and job and you listen)
- your exit small talk (where most people blow it!).

Let's start with the small talk …

Please don't try to cry off small talk by claiming you dislike it or are no good at it. Small talk is a necessary ritual and you're just going to have to bite the bullet and *get* good at it. Do you really want someone asking you 'why did you leave your last job?' before you've had time to take your coat off and blow the skin off your cup of stewed tea? An interview without small talk is like sex without foreplay. It's the warm-up, it's polite, it shows interest and concern for you as a person and it can also be very revealing, so watch out!

Very small small talk

This is the easiest to do as it's so ritualised. As formulas go, this is one you should never try to change. Originality has no place during this stage of communication as all you're both doing is filling in those small but ghastly silences in reception or in the lift. Remember:

- small small talk is supposed to be boring
- very small small talk is usually focused around two key subjects:
  - the weather
  - your journey.

That's it! Easy isn't it? They say: 'How was your journey?' or 'What's the weather doing outside?' and you reply. It's not a genuine enquiry or display of interest. The subject is deliberately simple to make it easy for you to answer while getting into the lift, navigating through doorways, playing with your visitor's security pass or gawping at the disgusting murals on the corridor walls.

However, your answer must sound positive. This is not an invitation to do the British thing, i.e. moan, as it could make you look instantly negative.

Tempting though it might be, you should also avoid curt, one-word answers like 'fine' or 'OK, thanks' unless you want to sound like a personality void.

If it's 'How was your journey?' your ideal answer will start with 'Fine, thanks …' and then continue with some detail about the traffic being easier than you expected or the great view from the train carriage. If you tell the truth, i.e. you only just made it by the skin of your teeth after being crushed underground by a horde of antiperspirant refuseniks, then your host is likely to see you as a whinger and expect lateness on a regular basis should you be given the job.

If it's 'What's the weather doing?' tell them either 'It's cleared up and is getting sunny now' or 'The snow/sleet always makes me think of Christmas' or 'There were a few spots of rain but I managed to dodge them.' However lousy the weather, try to keep it positive without sounding too much like Julie Andrews on Prozac.

Small talk

Think of this as like peeling an onion. Socially, layers get removed until you both find something in common and then you begin to bond and become friends or lovers. In business, bonding usually has to be fast-track, with less emphasis on becoming friends and lovers and more on being colleagues. Not all interviews will contain a session of small talk but you should arrive expecting it, hoping for it and even prepared to prompt it gently if it's not forthcoming.

A good interviewer will instigate small talk because it relaxes the candidate and shows the company has a friendly face. Sometimes this section of the interview will have a choreographed feel to it, i.e. there will be a few small talk questions and then a pause and a palpable change of mood and pace as they switch to the proper interview questions. Or the interview might have a meandering feel to it and the chat could possibly go on longer and bleed into the business side of the proceedings. Generally, you should use the initial small talk session to chat but keep much more to the point once the business side progresses. Most interviewers are time poor and therefore allergic to more waffle than is strictly necessary.

Ideas for small talk subjects

Small talk subjects are rarely random and you should plan for this stage in the interview as much as you plan for the rest of the questions. Spend the days before the interview swatting up on subjects of current general interest, like sporting events, news stories (unlikely to be politics or anything tragic), and general issues and events. Don't be led by your own genuine interest or lack of it. If the Olympics are in the news get up to speed on track events, UK medals, whatever.

Be smart and read up on any current stories that might relate to the sector of industry you're applying to work in. For instance, if your interview is with a fashion house you should know when the Paris shows are on or when London Fashion Week begins and be able to discuss the latest looks.

Holidays are another favourite, despite the clichéd nature of the subject. Be prepared to answer questions about where you went on your last trip and why you enjoyed it.

Although interview small talk might look, feel and smell like social chat, it's wise to avoid throwing questions back at the interviewer. He or she might ask about your holiday but asking them where they went could sound a bit cheeky!

Your surroundings can supply safe fodder for small talk. Although personal questions are a no-no, asking about the age of the building or who painted that mural in reception will be appropriate and make you sound interested in the working environment. Do try to be complimentary! Obvious sucking up should be avoided ('I just love these 1950s concrete workspaces') as should unmasked distaste ('How can you work in this battery farm?').

You're likely to be assessed during this small talk. Many jobs entail networking or socialising with clients, meaning your display of social skills might be evaluated. Your attitude and answers themselves could also be scrutinised. Did you sound positive, interesting and keen or did you just seem eager to get the socialising over and rush on to the business questions? Emotional intelligence is currently of huge interest to many firms and the interest is growing. This means firms are likely to be as interested in you, your personality and your communication skills as they are in your qualifications and experience. The small talk section could be your chance to shine.

Still worried about coping with the small talk stuff? Then get some practice in as soon as possible. If you're not used to this rather stylised form of talk ritual it will feel *extremely* awkward, rather than just *faintly* awkward if it's something you do quite a lot. The best place to hone your skills will be networking events and the more formal social events, like weddings. These won't provide you with an exact replica of the far more one-way type of small talk you'll be doing at interviews but it will kick-start the correct thought processes, especially if your normal response to rather dull questions is to answer with a 'yes' or 'no' and then giggle witlessly.

So instead of:

- How do you know the host?
- She's my neighbour (nervous laughter)

You can try something like:

- I've known her for what must be about four years now. She moved in here a couple of months after I arrived. I live at number 38. We got talking after her post was delivered to my address and we've been friends ever since. I work at the local branch of NatWest by the way, processing accounts. What do you do?

The skill of small talk is to keep your points concise enough to avoid narcolepsy in your audience but without being monosyllabic. Try not to close down the conversation with your replies. Here are the rules.

Think of your answer as something that will lead to further conversation, rather than the type of answer you'd give in a quiz show.

Stick to a 'Two-stage' response to open and continue the conversation rather than shutting it down. For instance, if you're asked where you live, instead of saying 'North London – Islington' (conversation closer), try: 'I live in Islington in North London (**Stage 1**) I moved there from Carshalton in Surrey a couple of years ago when I started work. Before then I was at University in Leeds.' (**Stage 2**)

Avoid moving to what would be the social small talk **Stage 3**: 'Whereabouts do **you** live?' or this could all begin to sound like a chat-up!

If the interviewer does decide to join in and disclose information, e.g. 'Oh, Islington? I live near there, I'm just up the road in Highbury' you'll need to frame a suitable response. Avoid clichés that will sound like lies, e.g. 'Oh how interesting!', 'How nice!', 'Wow, what a coincidence!'

If you can move this type of response on with a more natural-sounding reply such as: 'That means you must be an Arsenal supporter!' then do so (but not if you support Spurs as this could be kamikaze). If not, opt for the easier response known as **reflecting technique**. This entails repeating back the key word of their statement and turning it into a question with your vocal tone, i.e. 'Highbury?' This will signal 'Tell me more' without sounding nosy or bored.

Leave a trail of breadcrumbs

As with all the subsequent stages of your interviews, the cleverest option is to be strategic. If you can employ Machiavellian cunning but deliver it with an air of honesty and openness you should be well on your way to success in any chosen field (apart from maybe the Church).

In small talk terms, this means leaving a small **trail of breadcrumbs** with some or all of your replies, so that instead of allowing the interviewer to control the subject-matter you can gently and subtly tempt them onto subjects or skills that you want them to know about. Get it? (By the way, just in case you're a literal thinker, can I add the breadcrumbs are allegorical not real, so take that slice of Mother's Pride out of your briefcase at once!)

Here's an example:

- **Interviewer:** How was your journey?
- **You:** Fine thanks. I have to admit, after the kind of travelling I did during my gap year I'll never take public transport in the UK for granted again!
- **Interviewer** (picking up on your crumb trail): Oh? Where did you go?
- **You:** Well I spent six months in Goa teaching English to the local children then the rest of the year helping out a world-wide charity in Namibia on their health education project.

Result!

If the thought of this kind of active and strategic self-marketing makes you blush with embarrassment, then you might need to remember: **Grow up! Get over it!**

There's little point sitting on your strengths and talents in the hope that the interviewer will discover them. The words 'light' and 'bushel' come to mind. If you've done something great, then it's up to you to make sure they're aware of it. Most interviewers will see several candidates during the course of one day. Often this means they just don't have the time, nous or even energy to dig around hoping something extraordinarily wonderful pops up. The best you can sometimes expect will be the non-specific question: 'Tell me about yourself.' What you're unlikely to hear is: 'Have you ever done any great charity work in Goa or Namibia?'

The small talk section of your interview is a great self-marketing opportunity and you should see it as such. I've run many role-play sessions for interview candidates and seen the huge difference between those who can nail it during the small talk and those who come across as monosyllabic sociopaths. Here's a rough transcript of one role-play I acted out with someone applying for partnership in a large, glossy financial company:

- **Me:** Hi, good to see you. How are you?
- **Candidate:** Fine thanks, how are you?
- **Me:** Heavily pregnant, thanks, as you can see. I should be giving birth any day now.
- **Candidate** (after a very long pause spent studying his fingernails): Oh, great!
- **Me:** And on top of that I've been suffering from stress as well.
- **Candidate** (after an even longer pause, during which 10 tons of tumbleweed could have blown through the room): I see. Good, good.

I know this was caused by nerves, but it should never, ever happen. It would have been inexcusable communication behaviour from a first-time jobseeker but from someone who would be expected to charm, impress and possibly socialise with clients it was ridiculous. **Emotional intelligence** is vital. People don't want robots working for them, they want communicators. About 80–90% of problems in the workplace are caused by poor communications or poor communicators. Do you really think they want to add yet another rubbish speaker to that mix?

HOW TO GET INTO THE INTERVIEW CONVERSATION OR DISCUSSION WITHOUT INTERRUPTING

Argyle (1975) defined ways people signal they're giving up the floor to another speaker:

- ending a sentence
- raising or lowering intonation of last word
- drawing out last syllable
- leaving a sentence unfinished to invite a continuation: 'I was going to pop out for lunch, but ...'
- body movements such as ceasing hand gestures, lifting head, sitting back, looking directly at listener.

IN A NUTSHELL

- Good communication starts with effective listening. Train yourself to use active listening techniques.
- Your vocal tone can suffer through nerves or lack of use. Try tonal training exercises like reading out loud to ensure your voice is easy to listen to and understand at your interview.
- Projection exercises will help prevent mumbling or too-quiet speech.
- Remember the power of words – use high-impact speech, avoiding waffle, fillers or jargon.
- Avoid the **red rag** words than can cause conflict.
- Use **widthways planning** to structure your speech.
- Learn how to use small talk to create instant rapport.

9 THE AFFINITY PROCESS

Getting people to like you or approve of you

Is it possible to make people like you and approve of you? This chapter shows that it is. Using psychological techniques you'll learn how to:

- take practical steps to up your **instant likeability** rating
- avoid the 'I get better as I warm up' take on interviews and presentations
- persuade and influence more effectively.

First impressions

You know it's important to get your interviewer/s to like you during your interview. You probably think that being liked or approved of is something that just 'happens'. But is it? Is it possible to take active steps to make yourself more likeable and to help an interviewer to approve of you and your personality?

For most of us, being liked is something we take for granted and in this case it is quite appropriate to blame your parents for any laziness in your approach. Why? Well, it's probable and likely your parents gave you the gift of unconditional love. Your siblings may have done the same. It's all to do with love ties – no matter how much you might argue and fight with your family, it's likely they'll be there for you when the chips are down!

All this parental approval might have been great for your ego but not so good for growing your likeability skills. While you were tiny, you also had the advantage of cuteness. Babies and small children look and sound cute as part of their survival mechanism. When you were small everyone who saw you was probably nice to you, ooh-ing and ah-ing over your cot and smiling over everything little thing you did. This could have led to you expecting approval as an automatic right.

I bet you don't look quite so cute now, do you? If you shout and yell now and act demanding I doubt other people smile at you and tickle you under the chin, do they?

As you grew, you started to socialise away from your family group, finding friends and creating allies at school. I hope this socialisation made you acquire and hone your **ingratiation skills**. These are the techniques you use – either consciously or unconsciously – to get other people to like you and approve of you. The trouble is, you probably have little idea of what works and what doesn't work for you, tending to 'play it by ear' most of the time. This random approach is not unnatural but it's of little help when you need to take a more proactive approach. How can you ensure your interviewer likes you when you only have a few minutes to impress him or her? What are your active ingratiation techniques like? How do you come across to other people when you first meet them and how can you ensure that impression is guaranteed to be positive?

Psychologists call this **impression management** – taking steps to create liking and approval at a very early stage in the relationship. Although there are no real 'givens' in terms of scoring a hit, you can improve your chances by using an increased level of awareness and by flexing your behaviour, without appearing to produce a performance of grovelling and sucking-up.

Psychologists Jones and Pittman (1982) identified five key strategic motives for impression management.

1. **Self-promotion:** persuading people you are competent.
2. **Ingratiation:** getting them to like you.
3. **Intimidation:** getting them to be wary of you.
4. **Exemplification:** showing you're respectable.
5. **Supplication:** getting them to take pity on you and help you.

This list is important to your interview preparation because it helps you be clear about your behaviour goals. I do hope you can spot which motivations are appropriate for your interviews and which need to take a back seat. I'm even going to be bold enough to add one more motivational factor to their list:

Sexuality: getting them to find you physically attractive and desirable.

Your childhood **self-promotions** were probably quite basic. Most children tend to focus on the skills of **intimidation** (playground bullies who rule by fear – often very popular for obvious reasons!) or **supplication** (looking needy and vulnerable in a bid to get help and protection).

When you got older you probably noticed there was huge value in the sixth factor too, and added **sexuality** to your limited repertoire.

Hence the tendency to grasp at behavioural straws when we suddenly want to be liked or gain approval in the workplace. Without planning, your core **ingratiation** behaviours during your interviews might be any of the following.

Taking a challenging, quasi-aggressive approach in a bid to impress the interviewer(s) via your strength of character. This also includes refusing to modify either your appearance or your behaviour to create rapport.

Using several verbal or body language cues to evoke sympathy and kindness. This can include telling your interviewer you feel nervous before you start or employing submissive signals like hand-wringing, body barriers and even nervous laughter. Many of these cues are what's called **pseudo-infantile re-motivators**. In ape terms it means you act like a submissive ape employing childish behaviours in a bid to gain sympathy, rather than be attacked by a more dominant ape.

Flirting to gain approval. This can involve body language cues like leg-crossing, eye-flashing or self-touch, or paying personal compliments or even dressing in a way to attract sexual attention. In ape terms these would be called **pseudo-sexual re-motivators**, when the submissive ape uses sexual displays like showing off its bottom in a bid to distract the more aggressive ape from thoughts of fight. And don't pretend you've never tried it! (I'm not referring to waving your bottom about in the air but I do mean wearing a higher heel or using that extra splash of cologne now and again.)

However successful techniques of **intimidation**, **supplication** and **sexuality** might be if you're an ape in danger of being attacked by a bigger ape, I think you'll agree that they're not exactly top drawer when you're hoping to achieve success during a job interview. All three come with high risks. **Intimidation** can lead to conflict and active dislike, **supplication** can create annoyance rather than sympathy and **sexuality** might get you a date rather than a new job. Better then to focus on the skills of **self-promotion**, **ingratiation**, and **exemplification**!

Self-promotion

This will be a two fold attack, backed up with all the confident body language techniques you learned in Chapter 6. Your CV will provide the written evidence and then it's all down to your answers to their questions, which we'll deal with Chapter 11.

Exemplification

This is offering evidence and proof that you're a 'good egg' – you have a sound moral code and know how to behave around others. This will be where you promote qualities such as honesty, integrity and trustworthiness. One key phrase is constant throughout this book and I'm going to remind you of it here again: show – don't tell. Feel free to let your interviewer know that you are a model of integrity, but make sure you can back your words up with proof, otherwise they are just useless opinions!

Ingratiation

Psychologists have studied exactly what it is that can make us likeable to other people and E. Jones (1990) came up with the following results. Although they would need to be tailored for the workplace, this list of behaviours is an invaluable guide to the skills you'll need to employ. Fast-track rapport building is a crucial factor for interview success. Unlike social friends, an interviewer will need to approve of you immediately, as there's no real warm-up during the space of what could be less than an hour. Never expect people at an interview to like you better as they get to know you – it's probable that they just won't bother, especially if their initial impression is negative.

Jones's strategic self-presentation strategies

Agreeing with their opinions. I know this might make you sound like a brown-noser but being strategic means making it credible by seeming to agree on big issues while taking risks and showing any disagreement over trivial issues and balancing forceful agreement with weak agreement. During an interview this could mean making positive remarks about public transport even when the interviewer has suggested it can be unreliable, as in: 'I know what you mean but I'm lucky. My local line has a good record for time-keeping' (mild disagreement over a relatively trivial issue), rather than 'I'm against large companies that make massive profits' (when talking to a large company) or 'No, I disagree. I think leadership is all about making sure people do what they're told, not coaching and mentoring.'

Being selectively modest. This doesn't mean talking yourself down at every opportunity, but it does mean putting yourself down in areas that don't matter much to the job you're applying for. 'I'm pretty bad at karaoke' would be fine then (unless musical skill is a requirement for the job!) but 'I can never get out of bed in the mornings' or 'I don't know how I got my last job – just sheer luck, I suppose!' would not!

Trying to avoid looking desperate for others' approval. We're usually embarrassed or turned off by overt acts of flattery or sucking up.

Basking in reflected glory. It's better to make casual reference to your association with winners than with losers.

Here are some I prepared earlier

Your ingratiation techniques don't have to stop there! Here's another list for you to use. These qualities have been proven to create a favourable impression at interviews.

- **Altruism** or helping the interviewer: this can be a small act such as opening the door or passing some documents that have gone out of reach, or something more significant like telling a manager who is way too busy that you'd be happy to handle some of their paperwork or calls.
- **Status appropriateness:** getting the status signal right (see Chapter 6).
- **Communication etiquette:** sounding polite and co-operative, not interrupting or butting in to make your point.
- **Confidence:** looking comfortable and happy in your own skin, but not arrogant or lacking in respect.
- **Enthusiasm:** looking keen and dynamic.
- **Humour and happiness:** using humour to create bonding, but only when it's appropriate. No joke-telling or sniggering at the wrong moment!
- **Disclosure:** telling some honest and open information about yourself.
- **Creating feelings of rapport:** giving a good handshake, smiling with your eyes as well as your mouth, using names, and subtly talking as if you have the job.
- Using active listening signals.
- Looking smart and well groomed.
- Sounding positive and optimistic.
- Being punctual.
- Showing respect for the other person, the job and the company.
- Mirroring.

Re-labelling: how to change an old impression or bias

If your interview is internal – you're applying for a position inside the company you already work for – it could be that you come up against existing perceptions or even bias.

Stereotyping people in the workplace is common, mainly because it makes the act of understanding and dealing with people much easier if we can hang labels or tags on them. Unfortunately, this can mean opinions become fixed and any bad impression can become historical, dogging you for the rest of your career with that company. This unfair form of character identification is **labelling**. I have even known perceptions to be handed down from one manager to another, with opinions like: 'he's OK in an admin role but lacks ability to manage or the confidence to lead' being stamped across someone's image long after it would ever be appropriate. It can be very hard to change a historical perception and many employees find it easier to change companies, finding their career path much easier to rise up where they don't have to wrestle with preconceived ideas.

If you feel your career has been grounded in this way, you'll need some clever strategic planning before pitching up to your interview, then some nifty communications once you're being interrogated.

Find out what impression they may already have of you. Beware hearsay – it could be ill informed or misinterpreted.

Investigate and explore as many facts as you can. Did any negative perceptions emerge during a one-to-one or appraisal? Was anything written down or emailed? Can you trace it? Sometimes re-reading a document or piece of feedback can prevent your recollections being too subjective. Nobody likes criticism and it's a fact that we'll often over-react or respond emotionally, getting what is normally called the wrong end of the stick!

Is there anyone in authority you can ask? It might be a difficult conversation, but it's a necessary one if you want to progress. Is there a line manager you trust? Or might there be written records in your human resources department?

Can you take an objective, retrospective view of your work record to date? Forget all the excuses or reasons why anything occurred; what are some of the key events that might have created a negative impression of your work or behaviour?

Can you work towards a more favourable, positive view? What have you achieved in your career? It's easier to point people towards the positive rather than directing them away from the negative.

Understand your own thinking on any negative aspects. Are you trying to ignore them out of hand? If you were guilty of under-performing, making mistakes or lateness etc. it's always best if you recognise your own errors before moving forward.

Avoid what's called the **attribution process**. This means that when we do something that fails on reach targets or levels of acceptability, we often attempt to blame our failure on external forces, i.e. it wasn't our fault and it was out of our control. Avoid hearing or creating lists of excuses in your mind then and start seeing your behavioural 'glitches' from the other side of the desk.

Be strategic. Study their potential objections without seeing it from your side of the story. It's important to be aware of any misdemeanours or failures in your career and to know whether any criticism is justified or not and even if it isn't, to be aware that it exists.

Your thinking needs to be along the lines of:

- 'I know I screwed up the teambuilding task last year and that it has given a bad impression of my leadership skills and ability. However, since then I have taken on two other high-profile leadership roles in work plus a couple outside my job and I will use those as evidence of my abilities' not:
- 'I know that task went wrong last year but it wasn't really my fault as my manager kept making all the decisions. It shouldn't count against me. I know I'm a capable leader.'

Whether the problem was your fault or not, it's better to hold your hand up to it and find ways of moving forward, doing everything you can to dispel that bad impression via proof, rather than opinion.

Creating change

Changing negative perceptions can be a four-pronged strategy, involving:

1. **personal PR:** doing things and taking steps to actively change their opinion of you
2. **consensus:** providing evidence that other people have a much better opinion of you, e.g. using references or even getting them to canvass on your behalf
3. **top-ups:** this is where you take the existing impression that they have of you and add several layers of more positive qualities on top of it to create a more three-dimensional image
4. **congruence:** looking as if you mean what you say during the interview itself.

IN A NUTSHELL

- Don't take a passive approach to being liked or gaining approval at an interview. There are simple techniques you can use to double your chances of creating rapport.
- Re-address some of your current skills of ingratiation. Are they based on 'take me as you find me' assumptions or techniques from childhood? Learn and hone some more grown-up skills that you can employ for practical use.
- Never let existing bias or negative impressions of you stay around festering and scuppering your future success. Take steps to change historical opinions.

10 PRESENTING AT AN INTERVIEW

Not every interview involves sitting down in front of one person. As I mentioned in Chapter 1, you could be asked to get involved with group exercises, tests or even presentations. Business presentations are a common feature of the recruitment landscape and you could well be asked to present during some stage of your interview process. This chapter gives you a brief but very effective run-down on all you'll need to know to make your interview exercises and presentations sparkle and impress, including:

- how to prepare quickly and easily
- how to present with confidence and charisma
- why the idea of presenting should be seen as an ideal opportunity to shine at interview level
- how to excel at group exercises.

Feel the fear!

Although the idea of presenting to a panel of interviewers might fill you with terror (speaking in public often comes just below 'death' in a list of people's greatest fears!) it's important you see the idea of giving a talk as an opportunity rather than a form of exquisite torture.

When you give a presentation, you are allowed to pitch yourself to your audience without interruption (probably). This means you can give things your best shot, rather than relying on your interrogators to get round to asking you the right questions.

Fans of programmes like *Dragon's Den* will know that there is only one person in the whole world who can scupper your pitch – YOU! Presenters squirm, dry and they make stupid claims that get shot down in flames, they arrive ill-prepared and try to charm or bluff their way through and overall they fail to prepare properly.

If you have a recruitment presentation coming up it will probably be one of two types:

1. A pitch about yourself and the reasons why you should get the job; or:
2. A pitch to show you can pitch and present, i.e. your skills will be evaluated more than your content, which might be less specific in scope.

Whichever the purpose, your preparation will have the same structure.

- **Preparation:** structuring and planning your presentation.
- **Presentation:** planning how to deliver and which visual aids to use to get your message across.
- **Personality:** working on your delivery techniques.

What is a presentation?

It's really just another name for a talk. In this case you will be talking to an interview panel but instead of a question and answer format it will be very much you doing the talking while they do the listening.

You might be asked to present standing up in front of the panel or you could be asked to sit around a board table to speak.

There are two golden rules of a good business presentation: **know your goals and keep them in mind**.

Goal keeping

Your presentation is likely to be time managed, i.e. the company you're pitching to will tell you exactly how long you will be expected to talk for. To ensure you don't waffle or waste valuable time talking about irrelevant things, it's important to remind yourself of the point of your talk. You are there to persuade them to give you the job. This fact should help you decide what to keep in your talk and what to take out. I've seen candidates with a 10-minute brief who talk for four minutes about their schooldays. One candidate got onto the subject of his favourite hobby and spent five minutes waxing on about fly-fishing. Another spoke of his dream to visit New York with his church choir.

Once you've established that your point is to get a job offer you can start 'filleting', like filleting a fish. Imagine the backbone is your core aim or goal. Everything you choose to talk about during your presentation should attach directly to that aim, like bones to a backbone.

Imagine your point is: 'I know I am the right person for this job because ...'

... and then write down six key reasons that answer this question, keeping in mind skills, experience, attitude, soft skills, keenness and personality.

Once you have your six points (minimum) flesh them out a bit by adding your proof or evidence, e.g: 'I am a good teambuilder. Last month I organised a team to tackle the problem of ... and we completed the project successfully with good use of every team member.'

Once you have your bone created you can start to build your classic three-part structure. Most good presentations use this simple structure of **start**, **middle** and **end**.

- **Start:** tell 'em what you're going to talk about (introduce yourself and why you want the job).
- **Middle:** tell 'em (explain exactly what it is you have to offer the company and why you'd be good at the job on offer).
- **End:** tell 'em what you said (a brief summary of the main points and thank them for listening).

Work naked first

No, not literally! Working naked means planning and rehearsing your presentation without any visual aids and only bringing them in afterwards if you feel they will add to your audience's understanding of your points.

If you're an inexperienced presenter, or this is your first job I doubt you'll be expected to use lightpro or a flipchart. (Lightpro is a slide machine that works off a laptop. You create the slide show on your PC them plumb it into the projector. A flipchart is a large pad of paper sheets that you write on with a thick felt-tip pen.)

Scripts

One of the worst mistakes presenters make is reading from or memorising a script. When you work from a script you begin to sound too unnatural and rehearsed and the words don't sound as if they're your own thoughts. Never stand up with a piece of paper and start to read off it. Even if you intend ad-libbing you'll find it almost impossible once you've started reading off the page. I've even seen candidates read their greeting from the page: 'good morning ladies and gentlemen and thank you for seeing me'. (All sounding like a sat-nav!)

DO: take notes, but only bullet points to make sure you keep to your structure.

DON'T: hold them. Write in large print so you can put them down nearby.

DO: allow yourself to sound fresh, rather than contrived.

Never memorise a script. Your message is about you and should therefore come from the heart as well as the head, not just from the memory. If you falter on a memorised script, you might never recover. Allow your brain to think for itself!

Tips for perfect presentations

- Take a moment before you start.
- Create some space if your chair needs straightening or pushing out of the way.
- Get into a comfortable-looking position, breathe out and relax a little.
- Then begin by introducing yourself.

- Smile at your interviewers as you introduce yourself. 'Hello, my name's Brian Smith' won't work if you're looking down at your feet and scowling!
- Stick to the time allotted. It helps to place a small clock on the desk or table beside you.
- Never have anything in your hands. Put any pens, papers, or bags down before you start.
- Address everyone on the panel as you speak. Make sure you make eye contact with all of them on a regular basis.
- If one person asks a question aim your answer to him/her at first but then scope out to include the entire group.
- Use open, emphatic gestures – don't fold your arms or fiddle and never stuff your hands in your pockets.
- Remember that less is more. Make your speech clear and concise rather than rambling and waffling just to fill in time.

When you end your presentation, thank them for listening. Beware **denial gestures** at the end of your talk. These are like small explosions of relief once it's over and take the form of eye-rolling, puffing, grinning or giggling, childlike gesturing and even silly walks back to your seat. All these are prompted by a subconscious desire for liking and approval but all of them can also imply that what you've just said was a whole pile of rubbish or lies. Hold your moment after you end your talk, keep still but use eye contact. Smile and wait for any questions.

If you're using slides, do remember to keep them simple. They should not be used as your script and they shouldn't provide a running 'idiot guide' commentary to your talk. An example of idiot's guides is this one I saw recently at a construction company (names obviously changed!)

- **Slide 1:** a ten-minute presentation by Brian Smith. 23 October 2008
- **Slide 2:** why I am applying for this job
- **Slide 3:** where I live
- **Slide 4:** my previous work record *(in gory detail on the slide)*

The next slides were so full of words and details that nobody could read them, even if they'd wanted to (which they didn't!).

Slides like these contain details for you, not your audience. It's a bit like an actor having his script notes and stage directions printed above the stage for the audience to read.

Remember to blank the screen while you're talking. Just press the 'B' button on your keyboard and then press it again to bring a slide back.

If you've been asked to present on a subject so that they can evaluate your presentation skills, do take as much time as you have to research your given topic. You should sound as if you are the master of it, even if it's relatively new to you.

You can suggest questions at the end but please don't insist they wait until then. Some interviewers like to interrupt and this is their prerogative. Be pleased if they do ask you questions, as it means they're taking an interest and are keen to know more. Never look or sound defensive or even aggressive if you think you're being challenged.

If you don't know the answer to a question, tell them – but also let them know that you're happy to find out and how and when you can supply them with that information.

Put a presentation into your own words. Take control of your material at all times.

Tips for panel interviews

- Greet every member of the panel when you walk into the room. If you're shaking hands, shake with all of them one at a time and engage them with eye contact and a smile.
- Repeat each name as if you intend to remember it.
- Never assume who has the power in the group. A general rule of thumb is that the person who instigates postural change is the 'leader', so anyone who moves first in his or her seat and the others follow suit is usually the one making the decisions. It's good to act as if they're **all** in charge. Be especially careful about making any assumptions that the oldest male must be the boss. One of the quickest ways to cause offence is to keep referring to the big guy in the suit when you answer questions and ignoring the younger female sitting at his side (or even assuming she's the secretary! Gah! It still happens!).
- When you're asked a question, begin your reply by looking at the person who asked it but then widen the scope of your eye contact to involve everyone.

- It's good to take several copies of any documents like certificates, spare CVs or employer feedback (if you can) to present one to each interviewer.
- Thank each member of the panel and be prepared to shake hands again as you leave.

Tips for group exercises

By this stage of an interview it's your soft skills they're testing out. You could be called into an assessment centre or you could be asked to do an exercise in the company itself.

- Always listen to or read the brief carefully. The task could be very simple or hugely complex. Either way, make sure you work through it thoroughly, rather than rushing into action.
- Join in. Sitting back quietly isn't a useful option. They want to see how you work, not how you do what you're told.
- Be a team player. If you're leader show leadership skills but if you're a member of the team show you can listen to other points of view as well as work with other people.
- Some team exercises consist of two teams. Avoid jumping into competition with any other team. Often the two-team ploy is a trick and the task can only be completed if there is collusion between the two teams.
- Your communication skills under pressure will be assessed. Can you listen well and speak clearly and concisely? Can you make yourself understood by the rest of the team?
- Show your analytical skills off, too. Can you take a brief, check understanding, plan a strategy and emerge with solutions?
- Show what companies call 'can-do' thinking. Even if the task seems impossible, show you're thinking how it can be done, not why it can't.
- Use dialogues to describe your thinking. Standing quietly might look as if you're not joining in.

Tips for assessment days

Assessment centres are often popular with larger companies, who tend to use them to put graduates through their paces. Assessments can last anywhere between one and three days and can sound daunting! However, you should see them as a challenging way to prove your worth. Normal interview techniques can lead to some 'stars' escaping through the net because they're not good at one-hour performances and these centres give you a real chance to show what you can do.

One of the toughest assessments comes from the armed forces, who will often put recruits through three days of physical challenges, problem solving and the ability to think under pressure.

Financial companies tend to prefer tests like the **in-tray exercise**, where candidates are given one hour to read through, analyse and then prioritise a pile of papers. They are also fans of a much tougher series of one-to-one interviews to test financial awareness.

I know I told you to spurn advice about 'being yourself' in the book's introduction, but when it comes to assessment centres and doing things like physical exercises and competency tests it's rather hard to be anything but. It's the job of these centres to get behind all the hype and discover what you really can do. When it comes to physical exercises or competency tests, it's best to use your confidence and relaxation techniques and then get stuck in and enjoy it.

Please keep in mind constantly what it is that you're there for. You might be assessed at every moment, so if the centre is residential, no getting drunk in the evening or unruly or bad behaviour. Present yourself at your best at all times!

IN A NUTSHELL

- Know your goal. Keep your objective in mind and steer all your key points and persuaders towards it.
- Use a strong, three-part structure.
- Plan to use notes and bullet points, not scripts.
- If you use visual aids like slides make sure they're aimed at stimulating your audience, not supplying cues to you!
- Display good teambuilding or leadership skills at any group exercises.
- Keep your head – never panic and start to rush, compromising your strategy planning skills.

11 SURVIVING THE Q&A

This vital chapter investigates the type of questions you might be asked during your interview and shows you how to plan the smartest of answers.

Pre-interview essential work

Do your homework. Find out as much as you can about the company, its culture and its products/services as you can. Never assume. Some large corporations have a diverse range of products and it's vital you know what they are. Many firms are **umbrella** companies with a whole portfolio of products under their belt. You also need to know where the head office is sited. Is it run from abroad? What nationality owns it? Here's how to investigate.

- Look on the Internet. Most companies will have a website giving pages of information.
- Get or try the product or service. (Assuming it's not a Bentley car!)
- Ask the company. You could phone HR prior to the interview and ask if there's any material you could be sent to tell you more about the company. Many companies are happy to do this and many offer job packs in their advertising.
- You could also ask the agency, if you're applying via a recruitment agency. However, keep in mind that impressing the agency is as important as impressing the company you're applying to, so never allow yourself to sound as if you're trying to get them to do your research for you.
- Read the business and financial pages of the newspapers. Are they a plc (listed on the stock market)? If so, it's likely you will be able to get news items about their progress, giving valuable current information.
- Ask someone who works there. Do you know anybody who already has a job there? Or could you contact someone who knows someone? Ask around your social circle or see if you can quiz anyone at college or university who might know.

HOW HONEST SHOULD YOU BE?

A 2007 YouGov survey of jobhunters discovered 91% prejudge what employers want to hear and tailor their answers accordingly.

Check out the business

Don't just look at the company you're applying to, take a much broader look at the business as a whole, too. Who are their main rivals? What are the current issues? Who makes what and who does what? You should already have an interest or even a passion for the business itself, but if your knowledge is sketchy you'll need to find out more. For instance, it would be crazy to apply for a job in fashion without a good grasp of who designs what and who sells to what kind of market. If you want a job on a magazine, you should know who owns the group and what other magazines they produce, plus who their main rivals are. If your job is in IT you'd be wrong to assume your computer knowledge was all that's needed to impress. The IT department might be one small part of the business and seen as very much a 'support' role. What does the core business do? You'd be amazed how many candidates claim 'This is something I've always wanted to do' but prove to have little if any knowledge of the business or market when quizzed!

Keep reading while you're doing your company search – get down to your local bookshop and look for books in the career or business section that might teach you more about the market or business.

Get walking. If possible spend time 'walking the job' i.e. visiting businesses (some will even allow guided tours by appointment or if there's public access). Even if you can only wait outside, consider going there at either 9am or 5pm to see employees arriving or leaving to get some idea of the dress style and overall culture of the place.

Job or recruitment fairs provide valuable information, as do any fairs or exhibitions based on the business you're applying to. Do get along to any that you see advertised, even if it means travelling, as they can be a rich source of research.

Make yourself an expert on the business. Never go to an interview with an 'I can ask all the questions I want' attitude. Candidates who have bothered to find out about a company and business before they get there will have a huge advantage over the 'suck it and see' brigade!

ONE SIZE DOESN'T FIT ALL ...

... but 8 out of 10 companies use a 'one-size-fits-all' recruitment process, meaning they use the same style of interview whatever the job.

Shuffle your skills pack

You'll need to examine the skills and competencies needed for the job and then shuffle your own skills to create the very best fit. This can be annoying or even depressing if you have to sit on a skill you're proud of because it just isn't needed for the job. But there's no point pushing your incredible talent for training horses if the job you're after is mainly office bound. Or plugging your skills for leadership if you're being asked to work as a member of a team rather than as its leader.

It would be great if the only jobs you applied for were a naturally perfect fit with your skills, talents and ambitions. However, if you're prepared to be flexible for the sake of getting employment, apply yourself to some skills re-pruning or re-arranging to make sure the most appropriate are right up there at the top of your list, not buried down the bottom, underneath a pile of fabulous but largely irrelevant talents! Most job ads contain at least two vital sections of information, often listed under two key headings: 'The Role' and 'The Candidate', or possibly 'Your Credentials'. This is where they tell you in a nutshell how they want you to do the job and what they want you to be like. Read them, consume them, consign them to memory and work out how you can not just tell them you have these vital qualities but also prove you have them.

Read and re-read the job spec, looking for any clues you can find. There will normally be details of qualifications required but then also some character details, like: hard-working, reliable, good communicator, accurate, fun, caring etc. A quick scan down the current recruitment ads in a Sunday newspaper reveals phrases like:

- proven strategic vision balanced by a pragmatic operational approach
- you will be able to lead and inspire staff to operate in new and responsive ways
- diplomacy, tact and excellent interpersonal skills
- a strong and confident leader with energy and drive and a firm but sensitive leadership style
- your clear view will be vital
- collaborative and enthusiastic
- strong decision-making
- the ability to be flexible and positive under pressure
- you'll be entrepreneurial and able to think on your feet.

Write out a list of these words and spend some time evaluating them. If you don't know what they mean then look them up. Some of the words will be open to interpretation and this should ring warning bells in your head. If they've used terms like 'leadership', 'pragmatic', 'entrepreneurial' or 'collaborative', then my guess is that you'll need to define your impression of these words at some stage during the interview.

Alongside each of these keywords, compile evidence and proof of how they would apply to you. Think of occasions when you have been collaborative, etc. How could you describe those occasions clearly and concisely? Do you have any feedback from previous employers or even teachers if you're new to the workplace?

Be specific about your skills and talents. Research facts, dates and times. The more detail you can give, the less it sounds like opinion and more like proof.

- I managed a project in 2008 that came in under time and under budget and made a 45% improvement to profits by cutting back on expenditure and investing those savings back into the product.
- I don't yet have project management experience in my working role but I have been chair of my residents committee for three years, managing a block of 15 apartments handling the repairs and finance budget.
- Although this will be my first job in full-time sales I have had retail experience, working in a mobile phone shop part-time for the last year while I was at school. I was employed to give information and technical advice as well as working on commission-based sales. I was the leading part-timer in terms of sales in my last two months in the job.

All of these will sound better than: 'I know I'm a good leader/manager/ salesperson', however heartfelt you sound. Remember, the key phrase is: **proof, not opinion!**

Structure your facts: the four Ds

Keep to a simple structuring plan when you're working on your requirements/ skills fit.

Know how to answer the following questions and make the following points relating to job spec.

- **Demand:** the job asks for a core skill of …
- **Do:** I have that skill
- **Define:** I would define that skill as …
- **Demonstrate:** I can prove I have this skill by …

Transferable skills are in high demand in business. These are skills you might have that would add value to any organisation, both inside or outside your current culture. When employers talk about transferable skills, they'll be referring to such skills as management, motivation, leadership and experience of profit and loss accounting

Example:

- **Demand:** the job ad asks for leadership skills
- **Do:** I know I have good leadership skills
- **Define:** Q. How would you define the skills of a good leader? A. I think leadership is all about …
- **Demonstrate:** I lead a team of four in my current role and have done for six months, since May 2007. During that time we have handled two key accounts, both of which have been successful (add details, evaluating success specifically rather than subjectively). I motivated the team through changes caused by … via … (list of skills and methods, plus implementation).

Create stories and examples

Shuffle your **experience pack** as well. Think of stories and examples you can use to provide your proof. These stories will flesh out your points and humanise your experiences. Employees often like to hear these examples in story form as they can also watch you act out your feelings as you recount them. (By the way, the term 'stories' refers to genuine events, not the made-up variety!)

Stories don't always have to be glowingly perfect. Most projects and jobs come with a mixture of experiences, highs and lows and a future employer might be more reassured hearing how you overcame adversity than listening to you wax on about your wonderfulness for too long. Feel free to add a couple of 'low' points to your story but do make sure you end happily ever after!

Example

'I took on that IT project in 2007 and although it was originally only intended to last for a couple of months the task expanded in scope when the company took on an extra 400 staff in the Midlands and we found ourselves having to grow to accommodate them. This meant motivating the team to handle twice the workload. Fortunately, I've always been a very hands-on manager and when the job doubled in size they were all fully consulted about the changes and by the time the project was drawing to a close I was using every motivational tactic at my disposal from team-briefings to bribing with biscuits!'

Warning: Although I've used the term 'stories' you should make sure your examples are concise rather than rambling! Keep to the point. If they want more detail they can always ask.

Work on your hobbies, interests and experience

Do you have enough time to invest in some career-related experiences? Look at the field of work you're applying to. Have you shown any inclination to gain experience in this field before now? I once interviewed a girl who wanted a job with a teenage magazine. She spoke of her passion for the job and said she'd do anything to be a writer. I asked her about her school work and if there was a school magazine. There was, but she'd never applied to work on it or write for it. She'd never submitted one article to any magazine or newspaper or even tried to get as much as a letter published. Her description of 'passion for the job' didn't exactly match with my own!

Get stuck into the type of job you want as soon as you can. Any experience in the field will show genuine desire, keenness and even 'passion' for the job.

Look at your weaknesses

Good preparation means building up your strengths but it also means being aware of any weaknesses. Study your CV and skills next to the job spec and see where there are any gaps. Or look at any negative criticism such as lateness or career gaps that don't have a simple explanation.

Prepare yourself for questions about these. Never hope they won't notice or that they won't mind. Know what you will say if they're brought up and – if they're glaringly obvious – be prepared to bring them up yourself, along with an explanation, rather than having them break the deal without ever having been discussed.

Q&A

The main event at any job interview will be the question and answer session. For many candidates this will feel like the most important part, although our work on personal impact and factors like body language will have shown you this is far from being the case. However, it's still vital you put in as much preparation as possible when it comes to handling those key questions.

How can you work out in advance what you're likely to be asked? Well, most interviewers will ask the same questions to every candidate, just to be fair. They will have worked out those questions far in advance and each question will be asked for a purpose. He or she will also know that many types of questions are 'out of bounds', like ones about marriage and children that might seem to show bias against a woman in the job.

In many ways, this leaves quite a limited number of relevant or effective questions, which means it is relatively easy to pre-guess some of the ones that will come up, if not all of them.

Types of question

- **Personal:** asking about hobbies, interests plus general small talk.
- **Hypothetical (what if ...?):** for example, 'what would you do if you had a difficult member of your team threatening to quit unless he or she got a pay rise?'
- **Front-line or support skills:** if you are applying for a customer-facing post, these questions will test your client-handling skills and how you would deal with a complaint.
- **Technical:** specific questions that rely on technical knowledge rather than opinion.
- **Creative thinking:** many leading companies (especially IT companies) now pride themselves on asking creative-thinking or problem-solving questions. These might sound a bit like those maths-based IQ questions you had at school, only harder! 'How many times do the hands of a clock overlap

during the space of one day?' 'How would you move the pyramids?' 'How could you get your PC to function as a microwave?' Some companies even set tasks, such as building a bridge between two chairs using only paper and glue.

- **Definition:** asking for your views or opinions on skills and techniques
- **Pressure:** when the interviewer deliberately puts you under pressure to see how you cope.
- **Attitude and personality:** for example, 'Why do you want this job?' 'Tell me about your worst ever mistakes at work', 'How much do you already know about us and our products?'
- **Experience:** 'When have you done this sort of work before?' 'What training have you had in ...'
- **Checking:** 'I see there is a three-month gap in your CV. Can you tell me what you were doing during that time?'
- **Question:** 'Are there any questions you would like to ask us?'

Personal questions

When you're compiling your CV, try to pick interests and hobbies that will provide a useful clue to your ability to do the job you're after.

Never lie about your interests, you could find you're being interviewed by an expert! If you do lie or exaggerate, please make sure you remember what you wrote on your CV. Being questioned about a hang-gliding habit that you've forgotten all about could be embarrassing and make you look like a liar.

If you have beefed up your interests do make sure you can talk about them easily. 'What was the last book your read/play you went to?' are easy enough questions if literature or drama are on your CV but you'd be amazed how many candidates can't think of an answer to this type of question. If you've got anything like this on your CV, do make a mental note of a couple of good books and plays that you can refer to if asked. If you have time before your interview, I'd suggest reading a couple of books that you think will impress or going to similar films or plays, or even watching a few quality programmes on TV. Or do something if you've got a bit rusty. Go to an art exhibition or play a few more games of football. As a quick rule of thumb, here are what some of your hobbies and interests could tell your interviewer about you.

- **Sports:** good at teamwork, fit, energetic, physical confidence.
- **Reading:** quiet, clever (depending on your reading list!).
- **Exhibitions:** intellectual, creative.
- **Gardening:** quiet, nurturing, creative, calm.
- **Dancing:** socialiser, might mean late nights and early morning hangovers?
- **Cinema:** says very little until the films you've viewed get discussed. Avoid the likes of *Saw IV* or *Hostel III*.
- **TV:** could be couch potato with no imagination or social life?
- **Cooking:** thorough, patient, creative?
- **Animals:** nurturing, sense of responsibility, caring and reliable?
- **Hiking:** fit but maybe dull?
- **Dangerous sports:** reckless, daring, adventurous.
- **Collecting things:** passive approach rather than active.
- **Computer games:** doesn't get out much, low social skills? Geek? Obsessive?
- **Charity work:** values, generous, kind, honest.

Your gap year could also come under discussion. Did you spend it doing aid work abroad? Or backpacking to see as much of the world as possible? Can you combine virtues from each? 'I did voluntary work in Namibia … and got to see a unique part of the world as well as getting stuck in on the aid front' or 'I backpacked to see as much of the world as possible but I also learned a lot about different customs and cultures plus I got to see some of the climate change problems first hand …'

Most **personal** questions like this will be prompted by your CV rather than just general inquiry. Expect a 'tell me more …' structure, e.g.

- tell me more about your interest in rock-climbing
- it says here you enjoy singing and have even formed your own group. Tell me more about that
- how long have you had an interest in horror films?
- what exactly is it you enjoy about scuba diving?
- how often do you manage to get to the gym?
- what was the last play you saw that you really enjoyed and why?
- what book are you currently reading?

Answers to personal questions

These questions are an invitation to talk. By using a non-workplace basis for your communication it's likely the interviewer wants to see you relax a little while you display skills like enthusiasm and commitment. Keep your communications concise but fluent. Explain why you enjoy your hobby or interest and try to cleverly link it to the job you're applying for, e.g.

- I enjoy scuba because it's largely a team sport. Not only does it involve physical exercise and exploration but it helps understand things like trust and teamwork.

Spend a small amount of time telling them where and when you do your hobby and some specifics, like your favourite books, plays or pieces of music where relevant. Make sure you sound knowledgeable but don't waffle or become boring. Try to use a hobby that is interesting and even a bit 'different' and avoid anything too nerdish or compulsive: 'I have the complete editions of every Star Wars character cards from 1980 onwards.

Hypothetical questions

These are a little bit creepy but interviewers love them as they feel it shows them the inner working of your thought processes and offers some real insight into how you would behave in the job.

The problem with hypothetical questions is just that – they're hypothetical, not real. What you're being asked to give is an opinion and a strategy about an unreal situation. They rarely provide a proper guide to the interviewers, as most candidates will try to offer the ideal answer, for example:

- **Question:** How would you react if one of the partners here shouted at you?
- **Real answer:** I'd either scream back or cry or call my lawyer to sue for harassment and bullying, it would all depend what mood I was in or if I'd just had a row with my girlfriend/boyfriend.
- **Actual, strategic answer:** I'd use calming techniques like listening skills, repeating and reflecting and mirroring until he or she had got their point across and calmed down. I wouldn't take it personally but I'd do everything to help resolve their problem. I understand that people work under a lot of pressure and a little bit of yelling is only a way of letting off steam. The important thing would be that I could stay calm and defuse their anger.

It's safe to imagine an interviewer will be hoping to hear a response that sounds ideal but realistic and honest.

Front-line or support skills

If you're applying for a customer-facing post do expect questions that will test your client-handling skills, like:

- How would you deal with an unjustified complaint about another member of your team?
- How would you deal with a difficult customer?
- A customer has phoned to say she's waited in all day for her product to be delivered and no one has turned up. How would you handle her?
- You have two customers waiting to be served and another trying to get you on the phone. How do you handle it?
- A partner in the company keeps insisting you come down to his office to fix his laptop even though you know you can solve the problem from your own desk. What do you tell him?

Answers to front-line skills

You are being tested on two key aspects:

1. **Procedure skills:** how would you handle the problem?
2. **People skills:** how would you handle the person?

I usually refer to the procedure skills as your **physical response** – what you will do to resolve the problem itself – and the people side of the situation as the **emotional response**. This will sub-divide into two sections, how you will handle your own responses and emotions and how you will tackle your customer's.

Procedures need to involve detail, which can be tricky if you don't know the way the company you're applying to handles its own customer accounts. So use caution but don't duck out of taking decisions. For instance, it's no good saying: 'I'd give them their money back' or 'I'd guarantee I'd have the product with her by the end of the day's trading.' Although this sounds like the ideal answer to keep the customer happy, it could be impossible to endorse with action. One of the first rules in customer care is: 'never over-promise and under-deliver', i.e. don't promise things you can't make happen. For this reason most companies avoid terms like 'I promise' or 'I guarantee' – giving an absolute guarantee for something you haven't got total control over is highly dangerous. For instance, you might find the delay in delivery has been prompted by another company letting you down on delivery of parts.

However, just saying: 'I'd sort the problem out' is a major cop-out.

This is like saying 'I'd calm him/her down' to describe your handling of the emotional side of the transaction. 'How would you do that?' is the likely response, so it's best to be specific about your techniques in the first place.

Dealing with a complaint

Dealing with a complaint involves a six-part action strategy.

1. **Listen.**
2. **Empathise:** it's vital to show some concern for their feelings or predicament.
3. **Clarify:** if you're handling a complaint, it's always good to check your understanding of the communication before you begin the resolution.
4. **Solve:** this is where you tackle the physical side of the problem by letting them know what steps you're going to take to resolve it.
5. **Check:** asking the client if that solution is OK for them is important in emotional terms. An angry client will often feel stressed. By checking they're happy with the steps you're going to take, you give them a restored feeling of being in control, which should help alleviate some of their anger or stress levels.

Never tell your interviewer that you'd use phrases like: 'calm down' to an angry or complaining customer. These words are well known to make the customer madder than hell itself!

Another key customer-support/front-line staff question is: 'tell me about the last time you exceeded a customer's expectations'.

What they will be looking for is an understanding of the **exceed** technique, i.e. making sure you meet the customer's expectations on a regular basis but then exceeding them to ensure they remain constantly delighted by your service.

Some companies have an **always exceed** policy, meaning they put every effort into making each transaction better than the last.

Others have a more realistic and psychologically sound view, which is that you exceed expectations but not to the point where the client expectation level becomes unmanageable and they become impossible to please. This technique relies on emphasis on smaller touches, like good greetings, friendly conversations and being helpful and proactive rather than just bending over backwards to mop up after a problem or a complaint.

I'd suggest you show experience of both types of expectation exceeding. Tell them you're constantly looking for ways to add delight to your transactions via small but important actions but then give an example of when you bent over backwards and try to make it one that came as a result of your pro-active skills rather than a complaint.

An example might be: 'I spotted one regular customer who was looking rather lost in the conference area. I asked if I could help and discovered she'd forgotten to book a room and had an important client arriving. I arranged a greeting area for her in reception so that she could meet the client and have coffee served while I checked room availability. When I was told they were all full I rang our other site and booked one there. Then I found a cab and had it waiting outside the main entrance to take them all for the five-minute drive. I think the client thought they were getting special attention and service, being taken on a quick guided tour of our premises!'

Managerial scenarios

It's common to ask hypothetical questions during an interview for a managerial job. These will often refer to specific scenarios such as:

- A member of your team appears to be suffering from stress, although he denies it when questioned. It's time for his annual appraisal. How would you bring the subject up again and what would you do if he says he is stressed?

- Under what circumstances would you place a member of staff under a disciplinary?
- How would you conduct an appraisal with a team member who is getting good results but who seems to be using tactics described by other team members as bullying to achieve them?
- Under what circumstances would you get rid of a member of staff?
- How would you manage a team of home-workers?

Although it's always good to be flexible I would suggest you clarify your managerial skills and procedures before the interview itself, so that you can stay true to your values, whatever the hypothetical questions. There are three key considerations or goals involved with most of these scenarios.

Staying inside the employment laws: If you're applying for a managerial or a leadership post, it's vital to have a good grasp of employment law and how it should affect your decisions and strategies. Despite TV programmes suggesting the contrary (Alan Sugar's cry of 'You're fired!' from *The Apprentice* or Gordon Ramsay's bossing chef routine from *Hell's Kitchen*) there are many reasons why you can't just get rid of team members – you should be aware of all of them. Plus you need to be word perfect on health and safety guidelines on stress in the workplace and procedures for dealing with bullying and disciplinary action.

On the whole, your job as manager is to get results, which should mean using one-to-ones, appraisals and disciplinaries to achieve improved behaviour, not to criticise and tell off.

One guiding thought is that the role of a manager is to know the task and be able to communicate it; to form the team and manage performance and to manage individuals within that team. You should be referring to skills like:

- delegation
- prioritising
- motivation
- listening and questioning
- communicating clearly and effectively.

These are basic skills of management. Whether you have experience in a managerial role or not I would advise you to look in the Business section of a large bookshop and invest in a couple of current books on these skills to make sure you can list some of them accurately and define them effectively during your interview.

Examples of managerial questions

Q ***How would you give negative feedback to a member of staff?***

A *Your answer should involve an outline of your key objectives, which should be to improve performance, which means careful evaluation of how to go about that. Your feedback should be specific rather than vague, but not hurtful or tactless, which could destroy confidence or the desire to improve. You could choose to coach the member of your team, using your coaching skills to lead him/her to a valuable self-assessment, or you could use the 'tell' technique, cutting straight to the point and informing them what isn't working and then discussing how improvement can be made. You could also suggest how you would monitor the outcome and evaluate any change. Plus what you would do if any change wasn't as good as you expected.*

Q ***What are your views on diversity? How would you manage a diverse team?***

A *Diversity is currently a very important word in business and managing diverse teams is the subject of a lot of training courses. As a manager, you should have plans and thoughts about diversity in the workplace.*

Points to remember.

- Make sure your answer contains no suggestion that diversity can cause problems or be a negative element in the workplace.
- Make no assumptions about cultural differences. These tend to be prompted by stereotyping.
- Never use 'we' and 'them' terms.
- Refer to the advantages of a diverse workforce.
- Try to give examples of your own experiences of a diverse workforce.

Leadership

Hypothetical questions about leadership tend to be very challenging but rather broader in scope in terms of right or wrong answers.

The important thing is to work from experience or strategic thinking and to avoid clutching at straws. The interviewers will probably want to take you all the way through a difficult scenario rather than just listening to a couple of paragraphs of an answer. Sometimes leadership hypotheticals are nothing to do with the job you're applying for but everything to do with the skills of leadership.

One session I attended asked questions about leadership in mountain-climbing, based on the experiences of Chris Bonington, who is an inspirational leadership speaker. They went along the lines of: You have six people in your team, two of whom think they are the top performers and stars and are hugely competitive, yourself as leader, two less experienced climbers who are the healthiest and strongest and one member with an injury. Only two are going to complete the final climb to the top – who do you pick and how do you pick them and then brief them once your decision has been made?

Another more job-related question is along the lines of: You have been put in charge of a merger between two factories. They have been rivals for years but a foreign company has bought both and decided to place them under the same banner. Neither wants to speak to the other and both claim the other is getting preferential treatment. How would you get them working together effectively as one team?

Or you could find yourself being given a written list of jobs you would be expected to do as a leader and asked to go through them, prioritising, delegating and then describing what action you would take over the ones you have left.

Answers to leadership questions

A key point to remember with delegation is that it isn't abdication. I've watched many candidates merrily throw away tasks and projects to employees lower down the food chain and then consider their job is ended.

When you answer hypothetical questions like this, it's important than you take your time rather than allowing yourself to be rushed. A wartime leader in the field might have to make some very quick decisions to act, but in business you should assume you can afford to take longer to assess the situation and weigh up all the options before coming up with your strategy. Think long term rather than short term and let the panel know that is behind much of your thinking. It helps to sound a little flexible, too. One 'rule' of strategy planning is that you should always monitor the effects of your strategy and consider changing it if it's not working. A simple, bite-sized strategy technique is to:

- keep your core goal or objective foremost in your mind
- investigate quietly. Are there more questions to be asked or information to be sought before you plan your strategy?
- look at the situation from the other person's viewpoint. How are they feeling or thinking? What is their goal? Why are they doing what they do?
- take control of yourself. Self-management is vital if you're going to make a cool, objective decision
- plan your strategy
- try it on yourself. How would you react if someone behaved or spoke to you in this way?
- never expect a linear response. Look at every alternative reaction and where it would take you
- if it sounds OK, put your strategy into action, keeping in mind the most effective communication style or method to get results
- listen and observe and if it's not working:
- consider changing it
- evaluate success after it's over. Exactly what worked with your strategy? Too many leaders continue to implement too many strategies that only work despite their actions, not because of them.

Technical questions

These will be questions based solely on your hard skills and will easily test your level of competency. They might take you through a certain procedure or process to see if you know what you're talking about. As you can imagine, there's little room for bluff during technical questions. You will be sussed very quickly, so if you do suddenly find they've gone to the edge of your knowledge and out into the unknown, it's better to tell them you don't know (but with assurances that you're happy to learn or study your way through these next stages) than to lie.

If your job is hard-skills based, it's probably up to you to take a wide guess at the kind of relevant questions you might be asked and find out the answers before you arrive. If your hard skills have no real lid when it comes to knowledge of processes (e.g. IT) it would be wise to create a 'brick wall' of information on a sheet of paper, starting with the most basic stuff you can think of on the bottom row, then building up, with the degree of difficulty increasing with each row.

When you're studying prior to the interview please ensure all your bottom few rows are completely without gaps, as you'll only look foolish if you can't answer these simplest of questions. Then learn upwards according to how much time you have. Plucking a really complex piece of information from the top row while you still have gaps in your bottom row information is hugely risky!

If your skills and knowledge are sound, your only enemy might be anxiety or nerves. Read through the section on confidence in Chapter 4 to help make answering under pressure an easier process for you.

DO: speak slowly and clearly.

DON'T: worry about 'thinking gaps'.

DON'T: lie.

DON'T: ramble if you lose your place.

DO: ask for more information if you need to.

DO: give brief examples where you can, if you have actual experience of the thing you're being asked about.

Creative thinking questions

These are fun! Or maybe not if you can feel your brain over-heating at the mere thought of them.

Many modern interviewers love creative questions with a passion. They think they're beyond clever and rather mean and that the secret in finding the ideal employee is to confuse you with their brilliance while showing what a groovy and utterly cool company they might be working for, but only if they can tell you how to move the entire Andes to central Ukraine.

Examples of creative questions.

- How much does a football pitch weigh?
- How many times a day do a clock's hands overlap?
- How many uses can you think of for a paperclip?
- How many things can you not use a paperclip for?

Answers to creative thinking questions

As you can imagine, to compile a book of answers for every type of question would be impossible because the task is limitless. The most you can do is:

DON'T: look shocked, perturbed or irritated to be asked what will sound like a very off-the-wall question. If the interviewer loves them, then it's important you do too! They are clearly a business culture that relishes creative thinking and any lack of keenness to 'play' would have to count against you.

DO: show that you are working the question out rather than just sitting there stumped. On the football pitch question you should be working on a technique of weighing a patch of turf before multiplying it to judge the weight of the ground, then calculating the weight of the goalposts. Never sit there claiming either that you can't do it or that it's not possible to be accurate. There is a terrible term in business known as **can-do**. Companies love a can-do attitude as it means you like to solve problems rather than stall at the sight of them. If you at least show you're trying you should illustrate the fact that you have a can-do attitude!

DO: keep the corporate objectives and culture in mind. Even if you can't work out the answer, let them know that you are any or all of the following.

- **Not a quitter:** keep thinking and working on it until they tell you to stop
- **Creative:** keep a running commentary to prove it. They might be more interested by your thought processes than whether you get the answer right or not.

- **Logical:** keep that running commentary logical and practical
- **Able to think big:** the answers to questions like this are rarely simple. If one seems deceptively easy, think hard before you answer.

Definition questions

These questions are deceptively simple but are really aimed at discovering your depth of thought and your values and understanding of the role you're applying for. These questions will often feel very make or break as you will realise your definition of something like the leadership role might be very different from theirs.

The question is, how flexible do you want to be? If they show disagreement, it could be risky to change horses midstream. Perhaps your idea of leadership is something warm and friendly and encouraging and you realise theirs is more Gordon Ramsay. If you modify your opinions mid-interview, you're going to sound indecisive. It's probably better to spend time explaining exactly why you believe this is the right way to lead and how it has worked for you in the past.

Examples of definition questions

Q ***What is the difference between a manager and a leader?***

A *You should have a great answer ready and it will need to be more specific than 'One manages and one leads'.*

A manager does tend to manage tasks and teams but a leader should be inspirational, charismatic and able to turn the vision into reality. Leaders are strategic, but there are different types of leaders with different types of charisma and strategy. A leader can lead from the front or walk behind, motivating and supporting his or her teams. Before you attend your interview, take time to study and analyse many different types of leadership, from the wartime leaders like Churchill to present-day politicians, sporting leaders and business leaders. Pick out their key attributes and rehearse your own answer to this very important question.

In a recent survey on leadership among the top three things that employees looked for in a good leader were:

- trust
- recognition
- fairness.

Work out what steps you would take in a leadership role to create trust in your workforce.

Then think how you provide a good level of recognition. Remember recognition needs to be distributed on an honest basis. Over-praising a team for under-performing won't work, but if you're aware their level of effort was exceptional despite a less than stunning result, it's important to let them know you're aware of all their effort.

Think too how you will create these levels of recognition. A company-wide email saying 'Well done everyone!'? Or a more hands-on approach, understanding and speaking to everyone in the company or department, making sure you offer sincere and specific face-to-face praise as and when it is due?

And how about fairness? How do you create an environment where fairness is a given? Remember that fairness is usually judged on an individual rather than overall basis. One large company I worked with offered low wages but employees rarely had a problem with this until the day a list of the entire company's payments were posted by mistake on email and it was discovered some staff were earning very small amounts more than others. The overall low rates had never caused problems but the unfairness of one person taking home a couple of pounds more for the same job nearly caused a riot.

Q ***Define a customer***

A *Most companies refer to internal customers as well as external, so the term no longer applies to people who buy from your company. Even colleagues are seen as customers in many businesses, so it would be safe to suggest a customer is anyone you offer a service to, both internal and external and that the same levels of customer care should apply for both.*

Q ***How would you define a team?***

A *Remember a team can be permanent or temporary. Common goals is one defining factor. Teams need to be flexible. Think English footballers playing for their own teams who then have to come together to form the England team.*

Pressure questions

I quite like these and so should you. Forget hypotheticals, these do tend to give a genuine glimpse of how you would behave under pressure or in difficult situations.

Questions like these might easily be on the menu and don't allow yourself to be caught out. Sometimes they even take the form of a mini role-play. This is the type of scenario I'm talking about.

Question scenario: you have told your interviewer that you're very good at handling conflict or difficult people. The interview rattles on and suddenly you're asked about your favourite sport. You tell them you support Arsenal and one of the panel suddenly accuses you of lying. They've seen on your CV you're a Millwall fan and you're only saying Arsenal to suck up to the boss.

Or someone disagrees with an opinion you gave on the role of a leader.

Or you've written on your CV that you're good at thinking on your feet. The interviewer leaves you alone in his or her office for a while and either the phone rings or someone rushes in saying they need to speak to your interviewer urgently.

You might be having lunch in the company restaurant and suddenly someone comes up to sit at your table and starts to criticise your choice of sandwich ...

Answers to pressure questions

The point of these scenarios or questions is to challenge claims you've made about your skills. Don't allow yourself to be caught out! I've lost count of the number of candidates who say they're great at thinking on their feet or working under pressure who then either panic or sit immobile when a phone is ringing nearby, or who either lose their temper when challenged or are unable to deal with someone who is being 'difficult'.

Be on your alert for these 'trick' questions and remember it's your approach and behaviour that are usually being tested rather than your opinions. Keep in mind the behavioural skills that you know are a requirement for the job and make sure you display them. Remain calm, unflustered and polite and look for ways to take action if someone is asking for your help. If you've advertised your ability to act on your own initiative, this is your moment to prove it!

Another way to check out practical skills on the spot is when the interviewer asks you the following type of question.

Q ***Can you sell me that pen in front of you on the desk?***

A *Proof of sales ability will require a confident approach, so no looking awkward, surprised or embarrassed!*

Pick up the pen and study it, then ask the interviewer some questions before you launch into your sales pitch. A good salesperson focuses on **benefits**, not **features** – by which I mean there's little point telling the customer the pen is small and compact, uses flashy green ink and writes under water unless you know they are a tiny, scuba-diving leprechaun! If you list the things the pen can do, you're just listing the **features**, which might be irrelevant – or worse, a turn-off – for your customer. A few quick questions about their normal uses of a pen should enable you to sell them your pen by allowing you to list valuable **benefits** instead.

Another type of pressure question is the **leading** question. These involve being led or even manipulated into agreeing with the interviewer's premise even if you would not normally want to. I know the phrase 'keep your ears open' sounds amusing but your really do need to pin them back to pick out this type of thing. Questions like this can be deliberately worded to gain a speedy agreement but they can be a trick on the part of the interviewer to try to get you to say what is patently the wrong thing. The tone is often chummy and before you know it, you've been prodded into talking yourself out of the job. Questions like this should ring warning bells – plan your answer, don't just agree for the sake of it!

Q ***I don't expect you really know why you chose this company do you? I know we're probably just one name on your list!***

A *Explain to them exactly why you want the job, i.e. why you admire the company and/or its products or services, plus how all your skills and competencies will provide an ideal fit to the job spec.*

Q ***Describe the really monumental cock-ups of your life so far.***

A *Don't be tempted to reveal all your worst disasters, just for his or her amusement or for the sake of being 'open and honest'. Use one example of a challenge you have faced (not too self-created) and how you managed your way out of it. They want to know your ability to learn from and bounce back from setbacks.*

Q ***I hope you're planning better things for your future – I bet you'll be running your own brilliant business in a couple of years time won't you?***

A *They're probably trying to find out if you'll be leaving after a few months and taking all their customers with you. Let them know how the job you're after and the company itself will meet all your career needs and requirements.*

Q ***You don't mind if I ask about your plans for marriage and children, do you?***

A *It's easy to say 'no' to be polite, but remember you have rights. There is no need for you to answer questions about your private life in case it prejudices the outcome of the interview.*

Q ***I hope you intend to have loads of fun at your age before you settle down to the 9–5 grind?***

A *There's a strong possibility they're really asking if you're a binge-drinking waster! Don't try to impress with your party behaviours. Let them know that you do enjoy social fun but that you never allow it to have a negative effect on your career.*

Q ***This probably isn't what you really want to be doing is it? Tell me all about your big plans.***

A *This might imply the interviewer condones the fact that this job is just a fill-in but they could just be checking commitment or lack of it. If you want the job make sure your 'big plans' are linked to the job you're applying for.*

Q ***You probably don't like our products much do you?***

A *Join in an amicable-sounding slagging-off of the product and you'll never be offered a job. Let them do the sarcasm. Smile politely but never agree.*

The ideal response is to ignore the leading words and stick to your guns. If these questions are asked in the normal way: 'What do you think of our products?' 'Have you ever made any really great mistakes in your life?' you'd know to be on your guard and give more appropriate answers. Don't just agree because they sound as though that's what they want to hear!

Attitude and personality questions

Of all the types of question these can be what you'd most likely refer to as 'bog-standard' questions. They range from the usual suspects: 'Why do you want this job?' 'Tell me all about yourself' etc. to the hugely tricky: 'How would your worst enemy describe you?'

Q ***Tell me about yourself.***

A *This question is deceptively tricky because it's very open. What is it they want to know? How long do they want your answer to be? The first step is to avoid looking or sounding awkward. Never pitch in with old jokes like 'How long have you got?' It's unlikely they're looking for a version of* This is Your Life, *so imagine what might be of interest or relevant to the interviewer. In many ways, this is like a mini-CV moment but with a few human touches. Keep it concise, chatty and friendly but positive.*

Q ***Why do you want this job?***

A *It's vital you sound as if you know the answer to this one. Never shrug or look vague. Tell them why you like or admire the company and how your skills match the job. I've heard many candidates use the word* ***challenge*** *as in 'I see it as a challenge for me'. Think hard about this one. Would you* *want to give the job to someone who knew they could do it or to someone for whom it was 'a challenge'? I'd prefer people to have their adventures into the unknown on their own time!*

DO: tell them what you can bring to the job and the company

DON'T: list 101 reasons why you will enjoy the job or be stretched by it!

Q ***What do you already know about our company?***

A *Rest assured they're judging your commitment, keenness and interest here. This is where all your homework researching the business will come into play. Prove you have a good knowledge of the company but listen actively when they proceed to tell you more.*

Q ***What can you bring to this job? or Why should I offer you this job?***

A *It's good to register keenness at this point, i.e. 'Because I really want it' or 'Because I promise you won't regret it' but do offer facts and proof, making sure you add your skills-matching here and show what you can offer the company.*

Q ***If you did get this job, how would you go about improving things here?***

A *Please recognise this question for the hot potato that it is. You are being asked to criticise their company. Never assume that they think there's anything wrong going on in the first place, and do assume that the thing you criticise could well be the brainchild of the person in front of you. Try to build from a good place, i.e: 'I see your sales figures in the ad team are good but I'd aim to double them over the next year by …' Or 'I like the way that team briefing is used to motivate and inform the staff. I'd recommend the introduction of daily briefings to keep that momentum going and achieve even better results.'*

Q ***What are your strengths?***

A *Avoid using modesty here, this is a practical question and you should give an open and honest answer. Make sure the strengths you list are ones that are relevant to the job. I doubt you'll sound arrogant but do avoid hyperbole, like 'I'm the best salesman in the UK'.*

Always remember the magic phrase: Show – don't tell.

Every claim you make about yourself and your strengths should come accompanied by an example or proof. Never just offer opinion. And never offer vague opinions like 'Everyone I know thinks I'm good at …' Or even the deadly: 'My mum always says I'm really good at …'

Q ***What are your greatest achievements?***

A *You'll know these already thanks to your preparation in Chapter 4. Make sure you pepper some life achievements in among the work ones and do add recent work achievements rather than stopping at your school cup-winning efforts. This is also your chance to tell of a time when you overcame adversity.*

Q ***Tell me about your weaknesses, or How would your enemies describe you?***

A *This is often the moment when a candidate relaxes, sits back and appears to enjoy providing interviewers with a list of all his or her faults. It's a very British thing to feel more comfortable during bouts of self-criticism than self-praise but you will need to get over it, and fast! I've seen more people talk themselves out of a job at this stage than any other, in the belief that honesty is the outstanding quality being looked for here.*

It would be wrong to tell the interviewer that you have no faults! This question needs pre-planning and some careful strategy building. You're not going to reveal the fact that you have a temper like a docker with a sore head or that you're always late for everything. If you're going to draw attention to your faults you should try to make them potentially useful ones, like: 'I do tend to be a bit of a work bore at times', 'I have been told I'm too thorough. When I get my teeth into a job I do like to see it through to the end.'

Q ***What will you do if you don't get this job?***

A *In many ways they're judging your level of interest in their company, not waiting to hear you'll give up and fall into a decline. It's probably best to be concise here: 'I would have to continue my job search but this is my first choice' would work.*

The question becomes headier if you're applying for internal promotion. You must plan your answer to this carefully. When someone else gets the promotion it can often cause difficult working relationships or resentments. Would you leave or try somewhere else? Could you work under the other key candidate? Are they in danger of being promoted over your head? Never make too light of this question, i.e. laughing and saying it wouldn't be a problem at all. You could let them know that this promotion means a lot to you but that you would work with any new team if you didn't get it.

Q ***Can you take criticism?***

A *There's no need to look as if you embrace it with every pore of your body but you should let them know that criticism is something that an individual and a company needs to encourage if it's going to improve. (Expect some sort of criticism to be thrown at you later during the interview to check your honesty!)*

Q ***Are you flexible? Are you happy to work long hours/re-locate/travel?***

A *Most careers will require flexibility but there's a danger you could over-promise at this point. Can you work late? Could you move to any country in the world? Be assertive. You could show that you expect flexible hours with late nights when necessary and that you'd be prepared to discuss a re-location or travel. It's good to show flexibility but be careful about over-committing.*

Q ***Are you ambitious? Where do you see yourself in five year's time?***

A *This question can make it easy to talk yourself out of the job. Not every interviewer is an Alan Sugar searching for his Apprentice! Some jobs require ambition but others don't. When you're investigating the job spec prior to your interview it's good to judge whether this is an 'ambitious' job or not. If they're looking for someone steady to provide constant support or skills in one role, they might not like your claims that you 'want to own this company in five years' time' or that you're 'after your job'!*

If it's got a green light to ambition, though, you could try something like: 'Yes, I'm very driven and I like to succeed, both on a personal and a corporate front.'

Avoid: 'Yes I plan to start up my own business in a couple of years' time', as this lets them know you're going to learn all the skills and then pinch all the customers or set up in competition. This is beyond cheeky!

Q ***Why did you leave your last job? Why do you want to leave your present job?***

A *Keep in mind they will be likely to side with the previous or current employer on this one so avoid criticising them or even an individual like your boss and never give away internal secrets. Whatever you tell them they will apply to their own company, so although it's important to be honest you should also be tactful. Even vague references like: 'It was a clash of personalities' will sound suspect and they could think you're a troublemaker.*

Q ***How do you deal with knockbacks or failure?***

A *Avoid the obvious hyperbole, i.e. 'I never fail at anything I do'. Tell them how you only really define failure as not trying or giving up and that if something doesn't work you will learn from what happened and move forward. Give them an example of how you have done this in the past.*

Q ***Why have you decided to change your career/return to work after a break?***

A *Do focus on the positives rather than the negatives. Answers like 'I got bored' or 'I felt I was being underused/wasting my time' won't impress or gain sympathy. Look for ways to advertise how you are already using many of your skills and are looking for a way to utilise them more or take them in a different direction.*

Experience questions

These questions are all to do with discovering how much relevant experience you have for the job. They might question you further about your skills or ask you for more details about work experience.

Answers to experience questions

Proof of experience doesn't all have to be work based. If you're a returner to work you can relate workplace skills and talents to skills you might have employed bringing up a family or spending time as a carer. If you're straight from school you should look at school experience and relate that to work. Here are some potential crossover skills.

- **Teambuilding:** raising a family, organising social events, running a sports team.
- **Delegating:** getting family members to run the household, running and organising student accommodation, organising a school magazine or project.
- **Motivating:** debating or speaking societies at school, motivating your children to achieve.
- **Leadership:** managing social projects, organising holidays.
- **Project management:** moving house.
- **Selling:** part-time shop work.
- **Persuading and influencing:** children can be the most challenging targets for this. If you've brought up a family, you should analyse all your skills in persuading.
- **Communication skills:** think of all the ways you currently communicate and the skills you use to do this effectively.

Checking questions

Are there any gaps in your CV or flaws in your work record? Do your qualifications, work experience or skills fall short of the job requirements? A good interviewer will address these, so be prepared to be questioned about them.

Answers to checking questions

Avoid looking or sounding evasive or defensive and do be pleased they've been brought up, to give you a chance to explain. The fact they're still considering you for the job means it's not an immediate deal-breaker.

Q ***Tell me about this six-month gap in your CV.***

A *Do try to be honest but avoid sounding as if you couldn't be bothered looking for work. If you lost one job and couldn't get another offer even though you were looking like mad it's probably better to show your diligence or determination than to pretend you just 'took time out'.*

Q ***I notice you don't speak other languages.***

A *Keep it upbeat. 'No I don't at the moment but I'm keen to enrol in evening classes if I get this job.'*

The current trend for employers is to look for the person and their soft skills first, i.e. find the right person and then train them to do the job.

Historically the opposite has been true, with employers taking on people with the correct qualifications and skills and then attempting to train them in qualities like customer care and communications. I always think it's harder to train in the soft skills because often you're working with people who need an entire personality bypass to get to the appropriate standards. Turning a sociopath into a 'people person' is a much harder goal than teaching someone with good people skills and communication abilities to work equipment or acquire more technical knowledge.

Questions, questions

You should expect to be invited to ask your interviewer/s questions, either at the end of the interview or during it. Most interviewers will steer these questions, either pausing at certain stages of the interview to see if you would like to ask a question or letting you know in advance that there will be a Q&A session at the end of the meeting.

DO: ask questions as it makes you look engaged and interested.

DON'T: keep asking as they go along, unless you have been invited to do so. Never interrupt to ask a question.

DON'T: ask about pay, holidays or hours. These are things you should know but they will make you sound mercenary and you would be better advised to find out before you attend the interview.

DO: make your questions sound as if you're keen to start the job, i.e. 'How many of these projects do we get to handle in one year?'

DO: ask about training on the job.

DO: ask how long it will take before they make their decision about the job and how you will be informed.

DON'T: sound as if you are putting pressure on them, and don't try to make it sound as if you've got several other job offers to consider before theirs.

DON'T: ask for an on-the-spot evaluation of your performance or chances of getting the job.

DO: remember that any questions you ask risk sounding like deal-breakers unless you word them positively. If you ask 'Do I have to travel in the job?' you could imply you don't want to but if you say 'I understand the job involves travelling?' you could sound much more keen.

Compacts

In real terms there are two types of information that you will need to learn about any job – these are called **compacts** or agreements of work.

1. **Written and agreed:** terms of employment contract like pay, job definition and things like location.
2. **Unwritten and real:** what you really have to do; who you need to suck up to; who has the real power; how hard you have to work; what the company sees as successful behaviour.

These lists should make it obvious that although these are the genuine questions you'll need to get answered, there's little you can do to discover the unwritten rules until you start the job. However, you should have a good grasp of many of the terms of employment (at the very least pay and conditions) before you arrive at the interview. So do think of your interview questions as pseudo-cosmetic, meaning you ask what you think will impress them rather than what you really want to know.

Handling 'illegal' questions

There are some questions that no interviewer should ask and which will leave a company open to prosecution. These are mainly questions that can be deemed '-ist', i.e. sexist, ageist or racist.

The most commonly asked but 'illegal' questions are:

- do you have children?
- are you married/getting married?
- do you have any plans to start a family?

There are very good reasons why questions like this have been banned from interviews. They can imply a bias because they are irrelevant but could suggest a tendency to assume a woman would be less likely to get the job because she might take time off work to start a family and raise children whereas a man is often assumed to be more reliable if he has a family to support. Either way, it is a question that you **don't have to answer**. Under European Union legislation, interviewers may only ask questions that can directly relate to the job being offered.

Age-based questions are also irrelevant, as employers are no longer allowed to be biased by age. The same applies to any **disabled** candidates – there should be no assumptions about what they can and can't do in a job. And any implied **racism** is also banned, with race never being an issue that affects the interview and recruitment process.

Most competent interviewers are well aware of all the restrictions and will ask the same questions of every candidate to ensure fairness and impartiality. They also know about rules on questions about family or marriage. Those laws have been in place for years and everyone should be aware of them by now.

However, questions like this do tend to rear their ugly head on a pathetically regular basis. Some employers even pride themselves on their regular flouting of the laws and insist there is nothing wrong with asking about marriage or family prospects.

The point is, you don't have to answer these questions.

The problem is – how do you refuse to answer? Being assertive is fine and you should feel under no pressure to be anything but confident about dealing with them. If a company is especially bad about using them it could – quite rightly – occur to you that you don't want to work for them anyway.

But – rights or not – it can be understandably difficult to make your point during what can be a nerve-wracking occasion like an interview, especially if you still want the job. Your best course of action is to use the classic three stages of an assertive response.

- Display empathy rather than launch into conflict.
- Tell them your feelings or make your point.
- Be prepared to listen and negotiate if relevant.

In dialogue terms this would sound something like:

- I know questions about marriage and children are probably prompted by friendly interest rather than bias but …
- I do hope you realise I don't have to answer them and that I would prefer not to
- Could I explain/give you more detail about my workplace record instead?

IN A NUTSHELL

- Do your homework – find out everything about the company and its products/services that you can.
- Shuffle your skills – present strengths that match the job.
- Look for clues about the type of qualities they value in the job spec or advertisement.
- Prepare to give proof of your skills and talents, don't just offer your opinion.
- Plan and supply stories and examples.
- Work on your hobbies and interests to add value to your talents.

12 ESSENTIAL EXITS

What to do after the interview is over

In this chapter you'll learn how to increase your chances once the interview is over by:

- writing a letter of thanks
- ringing to see if an offer has been made
- keeping yourself in the running if you didn't get offered this job
- using valuable self-assessment techniques plus asking for feedback.

Exit interviews

You might think your hard work and effort is over once you walk out of the interview room and that all that remains for you to do is breathe a very deep sigh of relief and sit around with your fingers and toes crossed, waiting for the job offer or a refusal.

'Who dares wins' is going to be our motto (pinched from the SAS, I know, but 'who dares doesn't care' as far as motto-borrowing is concerned) so you're going to be taking a more proactive role over the next few days and weeks!

You should have been told during your interview exactly how and when you will be informed about their decision. (If not, I hope you asked.) Here are some steps you might consider taking during and after this waiting period.

Make a note of the interviewers' names and the next steps they told about, as soon as you come out of the interview. Do it while it's fresh in your mind, plus take a moment to take stock of everything that happened. What did you learn? What did you do well? What do you know you might need to change? How can you go about changing?

Write or email to thank them for seeing you and tell them you are very keen to take the job. They might be deluged with applicants doing the same thing but – guess what – you could be the only one and it could swing the scales in your favour. I heard from at least two professional interviewers who said this type of behaviour was the deal-cruncher when they were considering two candidates and couldn't choose between them.

Do make sure you spell their names right when you do this!

If the interview was arranged through an agency, you should ask them before making contact with the client. This is mainly a matter of etiquette. And don't forget to thank them for sending you along. Phoning into an agency to give feedback and a polite message of thanks straight after your interview is a good idea. It makes you appear more professional and more serious about your job hunt. It also confirms you went. You'd be surprised how many candidates don't bother to turn up. Agencies appreciate reliable jobseekers.

If there has been a delay that extends beyond the estimated time and you haven't heard from the company, you can phone to see if a decision has been made. This call needs to sound keen and polite but not desperate, stressed or annoyed. It could be they haven't contacted the people they don't intend to take on and you don't want to be waiting for ever!

If a job offer is made your next steps will be spelled out for you, although if you're waiting to see if there are any other offers before you commit, or just need time to decide after seeing the company and hearing about the job, thank them politely and say you'll look forward to receiving their formal offer.

If you're turned down for the job, it will be useful to approach the company to ask them exactly why you failed to make the grade. This is normal practice and you shouldn't feel awkward doing it. The information they give you might not be utterly honest (many companies refer to notes taken but avoid repeating the more tactless feedback comments) but it should be an invaluable guide to help you succeed in your next interviews. Phone the company up, asking for the HR department or whoever you dealt with for the interview. Tell them your details (including when you were interviewed and at what time, they might have several interviews per day) and ask for feedback.

Digest what you are told, rather than arguing with it or dismissing it. I've mentioned Freud's self-protection theory in Chapter 5, and although being in denial might be good for the ego it's no help at all when it comes to your practical interview techniques. One company's weaknesses could be another's strengths. You might find another firm will view you as the best thing since sliced bread, even though you make no changes at all. Knowledge is always power and much of your interview success will be down to perception and presentation, so learn lessons from you feedback and make changes where necessary.

Wait until you've been offered the job before entering into any salary negotiations.

A job ad will usually mention a salary range, e.g. £30–40K. Go for the top end unless you know you're under-qualified and will need to 'grow' into the job. If the salary is 'ballpark' you should assume there is room for negotiation. Add 12% and see their reaction.

If your job interview has been arranged by an agency, it's usually forbidden for you to discuss fees direct with the client.

Look at the variables, too. When you read through your job offer there should be alternative elements on offer and these can often be negotiated as well as the salary. These could include: commission rates, overtime rates, bonuses, health insurance, pension, holidays, expenses or company car. If they won't up the financial offer, you might find you can arrange for a more tempting package of extras instead.

IN A NUTSHELL

- Write notes for your own use as soon as you come out, before you forget what they said to you.
- Always write a letter of thanks.
- Digest any feedback if no offer is made – it can be an invaluable way to learn and improve.

13 TROUBLESHOOTING

Although all of your problems will be dealt with in detail throughout the book there will also be those moments when a thorough read just isn't feasible and some smash-and-grab, 'Break glass in an emergency' advice will be far more appropriate. As someone who is allergic to equipment manuals, tending to skip through any step-by-step instructions to cut straight to the 'Troubleshooting' pages at the back when I can't get my PC/DVD player/steam iron to work, I thought you might appreciate a 'quick-fix tips' guide in this book.

Note: There is a massive moral lurking here – if I'd read all those manuals I wouldn't get into trouble in the first place. The proactive approach is always best, so I heartily emphasise the fact that you should read your way through the book as well as referring to your troubleshooting pages when time is tight.

I get sweaty at interviews

- Work on your inner confidence.
- Wear natural fabrics, rather than Lycra or nylon.
- Wear a jacket with looser armholes.
- Use unperfumed antiperspirant and take it with you, just in case.
- Go into the toilets when you arrive and blot your face with a tissue, don't rub it.
- Wash your hands in lukewarm water (cold water will make your inner thermostat re-adjust making your hands hotter), then blot on a tissue (no hot air driers) before spraying lightly with antiperspirant. (check the product beforehand to make sure it doesn't cause stickiness).
- Have a sturdy paper hanky at hand during the interview to dab your face if you start to sweat.

I blush easily or suffer from nerve rash

- Wear a higher neckline – most nerve rashes stop just below chin level.
- Blot your cheeks with a tissue soaked in tepid water just before you go into the interview.
- Buy a tinted skin product like moisturiser or foundation. Most cosmetic companies sell green or violet-tinted products. These negate the red tone caused by your blush.
- Men can happily use the moisturisers.

When I get nervous I start to stammer

- Ride out the stammer – putting pressure on yourself to rush your next words to compensate for the pause will only make the problem increase.
- Breathe out slowly before you start to speak.
- Use one foot or one finger (hidden, if possible) to count yourself in like a metronome. This will slow down the pace of your speech, causing less chance of stammering.
- If your stammer is recurring and frequent let your interviewer know you do have a stammer but that it usually decreases as you relax.
- Practise speaking in shorter phrases.
- Try to lose some of the physical tension in your body. Clenching then relaxing hand and feet muscles will help, as will pushing the tip of your tongue into the roof of your mouth – it relaxes the jaw muscle.

- Don't apologise: many TV presenters and interviewers have regular stammers but they use them for emphasis!

I suffer from panic attacks

- Always carry a brown paper bag with you – breathing in and out slowly into the bag will prevent hyperventilation.
- Take an iPod or headset with calming music or pre-taped messages to yourself. Use it on the way to the interview.
- Rub one earlobe gently for 21 days when you're feeling relaxed. Then the same gesture will be instantly calming when you feel panic kicking in

I suffer from shyness

- Forget the diagnosis and work on the symptoms. What does shyness make you look, sound and think like? Change these, not your basic state.
- Pick out other shy people who manage to do well and use them as inspiration.
- Plan all your key messages before you go on the interview. Rehearse them and make sure you've consigned them all to memory.
- Rehearse your small talk moments. Practise with friends and family.
- Know at least one thing you'll say when you arrive.
- Be active in communication rather than passive. Speak first at least once before being spoken to. It will make you feel more in control.

I can't afford to buy a suit

- Borrow one if you have a friend or relative who is close to your size.
- Hunt through charity shops.
- Several supermarket chains make decent-looking suits for below bargain price.
- Shops like Primark do the same. Try looking when they have a sale on.
- When you're buying budget, always stick to classic looks and colours. Black, navy or grey are best.
- A skirt and shirt or trousers and a shirt should always be suitable if you can't run to a suit.
- School uniform that's clean and well-groomed can also work (but not if you're over the age of 20!). Can you customise yours by leaving off anything with badges or logos?

I'm worried my English might let me down

- Don't bluff if you have trouble understanding a question. It's better to ask for it to be repeated than to give the wrong answer.
- Body language is much more universal than spoken language. If you look confident, polite and open your language problems will be less of a deal-breaker.
- Always show a positive attitude. If you're struggling to understand or be understood, explain that you English is limited but that you're busy studying to improve it.
- Accents can cause communication barriers. If you know yours is strong, make an effort to slow your speech down and speak as clearly as possible.
- Where there are regional differences avoid the use of colloquial language.
- Be positive. How many languages *can* you speak? Could these be of benefit to the company?

I'm worried I'll dry during the interview

- Write a list of all your verbal goals – what is it about you that means they should want to employ you? What experience do you have?
- Transfer your list to one sheet and make each thought into a bullet point.
- Study these bullet points before you go in, they will help to focus the brain.
- Never write anything more wordy. Memorising a mental script will make you less relaxed.
- Try to start with a small joke, it will relax you to see them smiling and relax your own body to have an excuse to smile.
- Enthusiasm should overcome memory loss. If you sell all your good points to yourself first they should be easy to access during the interview.
- If you do start to dry, breathe out gently and focus on nothing for a couple of seconds. This will re-boot your brain. Panic thinking will only add to the pressure.
- Think of a small, silly tune that you know well and plan to run it quickly through your head if you dry, to help with the 'nothing' thinking.

Sometimes I can't stop talking

- Speak in sentences, not paragraphs.
- Pause before you speak: it's not a speed competition.

- Never start talking before you know your answer.
- When one breath starts to run out, finish your point.
- Create verbal headlines: make your point succinctly first, then only flesh it out if you feel you have to.
- You have one mouth and two ears. Use them in that ratio.

What if I don't know the answer to a question?

- It's better to be honest than to bluff, so tell the interviewer you don't know.
- Pause before answering. Maybe you do know the answer, you just need more time to think.
- Reflect the question back to allow for stalling time.
- Apologise: 'I'm sorry, I'm afraid I don't know the answer to that one'.
- Use confident, assertive body language. Never look shifty or defensive.
- If possible, offer an alternative piece of information as in: 'I'm sorry I don't know about Japanese banking systems. I do have a sound grasp of Korean financial practice though.'

I can never remember the interviewer's name

- Create a positive affirmation: 'I'm great at remembering names'. It will help your learning techniques if you're optimistic.
- Repeat their name on the way into the interview.
- Create a visual image if possible. If her name is Heather Stone, for instance, visualise the flower growing near a stone.
- See the name written in the air.
- Or think of someone else you know who has the first name. Heather Locklear, for instance?

I struggle using eye contact

- Start using it with the receptionist and then use it again with whoever greets you.
- If you're kept waiting in reception, use confident eye contact (not staring) on everyone who arrives or walks through the lobby.
- Take it in steps – think one eye-gaze at a time rather than just telling yourself to increase your eye-contact overall.

- Introductions are the prime time for eye-gaze. Tell yourself you will use good solid eye contact as soon as you walk into the interview room.
- Then remind yourself that you will also use good eye contact every time you listen to a question.
- And that you'll look up when you take your leave.
- With each of these 'prime-time' eye-gaze moments count to three in your head before allowing yourself to look away.
- If you do need to look away, look down rather than upward or sideways.

I don't know what to do with my hands

- Rehearse in front of the mirror first. Pull up a chair and pretend to be in conversation with yourself.
- Avoid holding anything, like a bag or pen. Props will exaggerate any fiddling
- Prop your elbows on the arm of the chair.
- Clasp them loosely in your lap.
- If you're sitting at a board table, place your loosely clasped hands onto the table in front of you.
- When you listen, keep them clasped but when you speak, use subtle, emphatic gestures to endorse your words.
- If you tend to fiddle with jewellery or hair, leave the jewellery off or tie your hair back.
- Keep your gestures below shoulder and above waist level.

I'm worried they'll ask about the gaps in my CV

- Plan to answer difficult questions like this. It's the interviewer's job to ask about gaps.
- It can be better to bring any gaps up yourself. It sounds less defensive.
- Don't lie. Be honest but as positive as possible.
- Keep eye contact and open gestures as you discuss them. It will make you look more honest and comfortable.
- Be concise. Tell them clearly and briefly what you did during any gaps.

I'm worried about any maths or written tests

- Use self-calming techniques like breathing out gently and using a slow metronomic tapping of one foot to stop your brain blanking.
- Focus on the question. Worry can make you focus on the previous questions that you may have got wrong and the questions that are still to come. Discipline your 'Leader' voice to tell you to think only about the present question.
- If you don't know the answer, tell them and don't display embarrassment. Dumbing down by giggling or over-apologising will only make things worse.
- Interviewers are used to increased nervousness at this stage of an interview.
- Unless you're given a tight time schedule, take your time. Rushing your brain will make it less effective.
- Do brain-training quizzes, crosswords and maths puzzles in the days and even hours before your interview.

What if I'm late?

- Always ring ahead and warn the company if there's any delay.
- Apologise immediately when you arrive.
- Let the interviewer know that it's out of character.
- Keep your excuse simple and concise: the more detail you go into the less honest you will sound.
- Don't blame someone else: 'My mum forgot to wake me up/my boyfriend got lost driving me here' are too childish.
- Don't give any excuse that will suggest future problems: 'I couldn't find the place/I got the wrong map/I was hungover' will set alarm bells ringing ...
- ... as will a bland: 'the traffic was heavy'.
- Something unpreventable or unplannable is best. Gridlock traffic caused by an accident, train breakdown or some other low-level emergency is best.

I think the interviewer dislikes me

- If it's just a hunch, ignore it. Some interviewers are deliberately less friendly in a bid to make the interview more formal or to put you under deliberate pressure.
- Always be charming.

- Imagine he or she has behaved like this with every candidate and that it's just a test of your resilience and ability to deal with difficult people.
- If you're at an internal interview and know your interviewer, you could be right. If so, behave professionally throughout the interview and never return the dislike. Your interviewer should be professional enough to be impartial.
- Are you being interviewed to move from their department? If so, their dislike could even enhance your chances!
- If you know there are genuine reasons for their dislike, i.e. you've previously displayed negative qualities like lateness, rudeness or laziness then you'll need to prove during the interview that you have changed your behaviours.
- If you've got into conflict with your interviewer before you could attempt some form of agreement prior to or at the start of the interview.
- If you're being interviewed by a panel, it's probably best to ignore the problem. If you feel this person is 'picking on' you during the interview, always be polite and carry on regardless. Showing or responding with any animosity, suppressed or otherwise, will almost certainly count against you.

I lack the qualifications for the job

- If you've still got to the interview stage (and as long as you haven't lied on your CV) then there must be some other potential they see in you.
- List all your other experience and character qualities and be prepared to talk about and market those instead.
- Sound keen to get any missing qualifications after you've been taken on.

I'm over-qualified for the job

- Bring the subject up yourself. They might think you'll get bored or be moving on as soon as something more suitable occurs.
- Let them know why it's this job or promotion you want.
- If you know the job pays less than you've earned previously, you'll also need to explain why you're OK with a drop in pay.
- Tell them why you still see the job as a step up in your life.

I get embarrassed talking about myself

- De-personalise the process. Think of yourself as a product you're trying to market.

- Write a list of six of your best or most relevant qualifications/work experience and six of your most relevant other skills/personality points. Consign them to memory to ensure you push most of them, embarrassed or not.
- Role-play. Imagine you're your best friend being asked about yourself. What would you say then?

I've been told I don't make enough impact at interviews

- Make sure you get remembered – but for all the right reasons. A silly tie or louder voice won't impress anyone.
- Most impact is created as soon as you walk into the room. Walk well, smile, use good eye contact and give a firm handshake.
- Sound positive throughout the interview. Negativity is a very common interviewee trait. Stand out by being happy and upbeat.
- Freshen up your verbal language. Are you using clichés and jargon?
- Freshen up your vocal tone. A monotone will always sound boring.
- Freshen up your body language. Walk and move with energy. Sitting too still is like a visual monotone.

I've been told I seem too aggressive/ assertive

- Sometimes being confident and positive can teeter into arrogance or over-confidence. Balance your status signals to ensure you don't appear more confident than the person interviewing you.
- Avoid challenging or openly disagreeing with the person interviewing you.
- When you present opposing views do so after first sounding open-minded about their views.
- Avoid implying that anything the company currently does is wrong or stupid. You might be wanting to bring your own expertise to the job but you should avoid trashing current culture before you do.
- Don't compete by trying to sound more clever than the interviewer him/ herself.
- Don't slag off previous firms or bosses you've worked for.
- Don't use more eye contact than they do, or a stronger handshake.
- Avoid using terms like 'obviously ...' at the start of your answers.

I've been told I'm too blunt

- Does your straight-talking lack tact? Make your communication more objective focused. Ask yourself 'What do I want to achieve from this interview?'
- Never use phrases like: 'I'm not being rude but …', 'I hope I'm not being too blunt but …' or 'With respect …' They all lead to tactless statements.
- Pause before speaking. Even repeat the question to stall for time.
- Always see a statement or a point from the other person's viewpoint before you speak.
- Tact isn't weakness, it's strategic.

After a few bad interviews I get very demotivated and start giving up

- Think of interviews as a campaign. There will be different stages. One stage is bound to be lack of motivation and energy.
- Re-boot. Go through a list of all your achievements and positive points.
- See each interview as a separate unit. Carrying negative messages and baggage from a previous interview into the next one is unhelpful and illogical.
- Only analyse a previous interview to evaluate what you did right and what you may have done wrong. Learn to change anything that isn't working.
- Paranoia is also unhelpful. If you don't know why you didn't get a previous interview never make wild speculations.

I'm older than most of the people interviewing me

- You have age discrimination law on your side.
- Try not to confuse ability with experience – both yours and the interviewers'.
- Experience is only useful if it's positive. Stress that what you've learned works and can be done, not what you've learned **can't** or is a waste of time to try.
- Enthusiasm and energy are always better than cynicism.
- They shouldn't make an issue of your age and you mustn't. Don't make constant references to it yourself.

- Never use phrases like: 'In my day …', 'Of course you won't remember but …' or 'At my age …' etc. This is almost self-discrimination.

I might be too young for the position

- Remind yourself about all the positive things your age might bring to this job.
- Don't try to dress or act old but do go for a timeless look rather than emphasising your youth.
- Use good, solid eye contact.
- Try dropping your vocal tone a note or two: higher voices sound more childlike.
- Use rituals like handshaking to show off your confident social side.
- Take a good briefcase and a good pen, they make a positive investment.